C. S. Lewis: A Very Short Introduction

'Matthew Arnold praised writers who could see life steadily and see it whole. James Como has performed that service admirably by providing a brisk new overview of C. S. Lewis's life and writings. Como's book will be very illuminating for new readers of Lewis. But it also provides fresh perspective and insight for even the most seasoned of Lewis scholars. Como is concise, perceptive, and readable, just the sort of introduction one hopes to find in this distinguished series.'

David C. Downing, Co-Director and Co-Chair of Christian Thought,
The Marion E. Wade Center, Wheaton College

VERY SHORT INTRODUCTIONS are for anyone wanting a stimulating and accessible way into a new subject. They are written by experts, and have been translated into more than 45 different languages.

The series began in 1995, and now covers a wide variety of topics in every discipline. The VSI library currently contains over 550 volumes—a Very Short Introduction to everything from Psychology and Philosophy of Science to American History and Relativity—and continues to grow in every subject area.

Very Short Introductions available now:

Available soon:

For more information visit our website

www.oup.com/vsi/

James Como

C. S. LEWIS

A Very Short Introduction

Great Clarendon Street, Oxford, OX2 6DP,
United Kingdom

Oxford University Press is a department of the University of Oxford.
It furthers the University's objective of excellence in research, scholarship,
and education by publishing worldwide. Oxford is a registered trade mark of
Oxford University Press in the UK and in certain other countries

First edition published in 2019

Impression: 1

Published in the United States of America by Oxford University Press
198 Madison Avenue, New York, NY 10016, United States of America

British Library Cataloguing in Publication Data

Data available

Library of Congress Control Number: 2018958746

ISBN 978-0-19-882824-2

Printed in Great Britain by
Ashford Colour Press Ltd, Gosport, Hampshire

To Walter Hooper

Contents

Preface

C. S. Lewis was writing stories in his early childhood, near the beginning of the 20th century. Soon he was writing letters and poetry, and he would practise these forms—fiction, letters, poetry—throughout his life. Though becoming a poet was his first serious ambition, many other forms would join the array and lift him to fame. His first published work was indeed poetry, coming when he was a very young man, but his strong public voice did not emerge until the early 1930s, when he was in his mid-thirties. So we can see that Lewis has been a professional writer (with many voices) for one hundred years, a consequential one for nearly ninety.

During the course of his forty-five years of publishing (from 1919 to 1964) Lewis gave us forty books (depending on how one counts; people have added to that number by collecting and editing other works), some 200 assorted essays, over 150 poems, a handful of short stories, a brief diary, and three volumes of letters, a prominent element not only of Lewis's daily routine (with his brother's help he answered all the letters he received) but of his body of work, evidencing his wide-ranging mind and pastoral vocation as well as casting light on facets of his public and private lives.

That body of work includes a prodigious range of genres, from literary history, theory, and criticism (the teaching of which was his livelihood), to the fantasy, science fiction, allegory, satire, narrative and lyric poetry, social and cultural essays, and religious philosophy; and, of course, Christian apologetics—his explanations and defences of Christian belief ('apology' at its root meaning 'defence').

My own history with C. S. Lewis began in 1964, with his literary criticism. Eventually I reached *The Chronicles of Narnia*, a transformative experience soon to be located within Lewis's larger literary landscape of much learning, severe thinking, high imagination, deep spirituality, and an appealing personality. That is, coming through the words there was a distinctive, concrete person who exuded trustworthiness. Soon I realized that I must speak with others about him, so in 1969 thirteen of us founded the New York C. S. Lewis Society. Over our fifty years we have had thousands of members from all over the world and our bulletin, *CSL*, is among the journals that Lewis readers and scholars alike regularly read and consult.

The first study of his work came in the late 1940s. Thereafter that single drop became a trickle, then a stream, then—a tsunami. (Forty years ago I heard one publisher say, 'oh, Lord, not another book about C. S. Lewis'; if only he could have known.) Inevitably many puzzling claims would be made about Lewis (and sometimes about his friends): erroneous factual statements, insufficiently qualified judgments, honestly gained insights of questionable relevance, and wildly bizarre conclusions.

I found that the most famous Lewis, the writer of children's stories, took up so much of his reputation that it overshadowed the breadth of the man's achievement as well as his broad cultural influence. This seems to be changing. Now more than ever scholars, biographers, literary journalists, and 'public intellectuals' are paying attention to regions of Lewis's work that had been relatively neglected. If some of these writers go too far, for example by requiring that this book or that sermon bear too much weight of philosophy or theology, or by afflicting his work with trendy complaints, or by co-opting him for a cause, still I regard such excess as a small price to pay for a view of Lewis whole. Not without his blind spots, he worked from a broad intellectual and literary context, much of it no longer readily accessible.

For the most part this *Very Short Introduction* to C. S. Lewis proceeds chronologically. Since this book is essentially a literary survey, not a study, I thought it useful to include (much abbreviated) Lewis's own story, his life and personality being vital in much of his work. Thus each chapter contains summaries of works, some biography, and an occasional connection between the two.

I hope the reader will discern, if only to a small degree, the sheer *amplitude* that Lewis's friends and the preponderance of his readers found and find in him. Perhaps there is a Lewis for every stage and age of a person's life and interests, from atheist to saint, unlearned to expert, undecided to perfectly settled, with all manner of beliefs, allegiances, and dispositions in between. Withal it is easy to lose sight of just how complex, productive, influential, charismatic, and steadfast this portly, rumpled man was. We should keep in mind that he was very much his own man.

A word about the friend to whom I dedicate this book, Walter Hooper. Now and again there arises the question of who is the greatest authority on Lewis, to which my answer is: there is none, except... Hooper. And since he (very briefly) figures in the story, here I will say only this. Without him we simply would not have Lewis as we do. There were other 'godfathers' of Lewis's posthumous work and reputation, most notably Professor Clyde S. Kilby (who began what is now the dispositive Marion C. Wade Collection at Wheaton College in Illinois), but none as assiduous as Hooper.

At the end of this book are a list of Lewis's works by type, providing a selection of primary sources, with each title dated; another list of books important to Lewis which may guide the reader who cares to share Lewis's intellectual, imaginative, and spiritual interests; and a selected secondary bibliography that could have been five times longer. I am grateful to such a capable, resourceful, and committed community of scholars and writers—as well as to readers, fans, critics, and others—who share their interest in and knowledge of Lewis.

Two final items. First, I am very fortunate to have fallen into the hands of those who midwifed this book: Andrea Keegan and her associate Jenny Nugee, as well as the thoroughly generous and supremely professional editorial team at Oxford University Press. And this: if I sometimes seem to be an enthusiast that is because I am.

List of illustrations

1. Characteristic C. S. Lewis, in his prime in the late 1940s.

Chapter 1
Lewis on the way

C. S. Lewis sometimes wrote for a section evocatively called 'Notes on the Way' that appeared in an influential literary weekly review called *Time and Tide*, both of which Lewis would struggle against until the end.

Not long after his death on 22 November 1963, his reputation, at its international height from the mid-1940s to the late 1950s (see Figure 1), went into decline. Owing to several factors the recovery was so robust it would lead to the question that (especially in England) I heard frequently, 'Why all the fuss?' One answer is difficult to document, for it lies mostly in the penetrating impact of Lewis's work on individual readers. The children's fantasy series *The Chronicles of Narnia* (seven books, 1950–6) led the revival, of course, with *Mere Christianity* (1952, a gathering of his BBC broadcasts from the 1940 explaining Christian premises and beliefs), *The Screwtape Letters* (1942, a satirical series of letters from one devil to another), and *A Grief Observed* (1961, the journal he kept on the death of his wife) close behind.

He was an avid reader of narrative poetry. Spenser's *The Faerie Queene* and Wordsworth's *The Prelude* were among his favourites; but he would reread (and translate sections of) Virgil's *Aeneid* more than any other book. He would write four narrative poems. He would also write over 150 lyrical poems. In short, he was fond of writing what he liked to read, especially fairy tales and science fiction.

Images of the author, and of the man

The Christian writer, religious and social philosopher, teacher, conversationalist, and general man of letters—imaginative and rational, authoritative and familiar, witty though intellectually severe, combative and mild, certain yet somehow restrained, defiant and unfashionable while also gregarious, good-humoured, and popular to the point of being charismatic—this man proved hard to resist.

Still, any great figure's reputation is tenuous and somehow false. Now biographies of Lewis abound; different media treatments—television and feature films of *The Chronicles*, television documentaries such as *The Question of God*, theatre productions including *The Great Divorce*, *The Screwtape Letters*, and *Shadowlands*, about his love affair with and marriage to Joy Davidman Gresham (also a successful feature film), and radio dramas of *The Chronicles*—these saturate a corner of general culture; President George H. W. Bush's tagline, 'a thousand points of light', was taken from *The Magician's Nephew* (one of the Narnia books), his Lewis works were at the bedside of Pope Saint John Paul II, and tourists take guided tours of his Oxford haunts and home, the Kilns.

In the novel *Bonfire of the Vanities*, Tom Wolfe could bandy about his name because (as he wrote to me) he needed a universally recognized moral authority at a certain point in his plot. Novelists Robertson Davies and Walker Percy would do the same. Translations of his books proliferate, scholarly books on him and his work constitute an industry, websites thrive (as do societies, institutes, and foundations), spin-offs and rip-offs have been tried, toys (I've even heard of a Lewis bobble-head doll) are on the market, a statue of a man entering the famous wardrobe stands in Belfast, and he has a dedicated plaque in

Westminster Abbey at Poets' Corner. Apparently a barrier has been breached; his many eminently accessible voices continue to convey clear argument, sound judgement, absorbing stories, uncommon psychological insight, and beckoning images of hope.

But C. S. Lewis is no longer a contemporary figure, and among the more interesting implications of that truth is the entrance into our lexicon of 'Lewisian'. Of course, out of context it is impossible to say which C. S. Lewis the adjective refers to: avuncular Narnian, plausible apologist, penetrating religious thinker (apologist aside), promethean literary historian and critic, combative journalist and book reviewer, broadcaster, preacher, university personality, incantatory story-teller, debater, conversationalist and friend, or comforting letter-writer. (The definitive edition of Lewis's letters, in three volumes, is *C. S. Lewis: Collected Letters*, edited by Walter Hooper, with each volume amply annotated and including a Biographical Appendix and an exhaustively detailed index: 3,999 pages in all.) So, when considering Lewis proper, we should not forget a famous warning from John Keats in a letter of 3 May 1819, to his brother George: 'A man's life of any worth is a continual allegory—and very few eyes can see the mystery of life—a life like the Scriptures, figurative'.

For example, Lewis could be quirky. When Clive Staples (thus the initials) was a very young child his dog Jacksie was killed by a coach in front of his house. At that moment the boy pointed to himself and said, 'Jacksie', meaning that he would be called by that name. That is how C. S. Lewis became 'Jack' to his family and friends for the rest of his life. A few years later Jacksie announced to his parents that he was prejudiced against the French. 'But why?' asked his father. 'Well, if I knew why it wouldn't be a prejudice, would it?' he answered, rationally, precociously, and cheekily.

He would give money to beggars over the objection of his great friend Tolkien. 'Jack', Tolkien would say, 'he's only going to drink it up', and Lewis would answer, 'well, Tollers, that's exactly what

3

I was going to do with it'. Later in his life he would establish what he called the Agape Fund, an instrument whereby he could give away nearly 70 per cent of his income, anonymously, and no matter how it compromised him financially (which it would).

Although his mother held a degree in mathematics his own maths skills were poor that he almost did not get into Oxford (and couldn't really manage his chequebook: he and his brother, Warren, often thought they were going broke). On the other hand, he could remember almost everything he read, not generally but word for word. When an undergraduate complained of not being able to remember what he read, Lewis said the opposite, too, was burdensome: quite a claim. Someone would then choose a book at random, read part of a page, and Lewis would complete that page from memory: a parlour trick, perhaps, but one he would repeat.

And yet Lewis apparently had some trouble with spelling, as the manuscript of *The Screwtape Letters* reveals. In the book we read that Wormwood, the apprentice devil, should have his 'patient' (that's one of us) 'fix' his attention on his own feelings. But in the manuscript Lewis first wrote 'revit', misspelling 'rivet'. He tried again, and again failed. Finally, after getting it right but unsure of himself, he crossed out the correct attempt and wrote 'FIX'.

Animals delighted Lewis. At the height of his fame he owned (a term Lewis would dispute) one Mr Papworth, a dog who in his senility would not eat standing still *or* if anyone watched. So Lewis would walk along the lane tossing food over his shoulder with Mr Papworth gobbling it up as he followed. Or this, as his brother recounted: 'It is said that Jack once took a guest for an early morning walk on the Magdalen College grounds...after a very wet night. Presently the guest brought his attention to a curious lump of cloth hanging on a bush [apparently a nest for field mice]. "That looks like my hat," said Jack; then, joyfully, "*It is my hat*." And, clapping the sodden mass on his head, he continued his walk.' Given his fondness for mice, were the hat not empty he very well might have kept them as pets.

Will, words, and character

These quirks (though alms-giving is hardly that) are remarkable and charming, and more. Like a boy naming himself and declaring a prejudice, they are purposeful; that is, they are the results of an act of will, for Lewis was a wilful man, even 'a genius of the will', according to his 'second friend' Owen Barfield. And the application of that will would pay dividends (as well as debits, as we shall see further on). At a certain point, reports Barfield, he 'deliberately ceased to take any interest in himself except as a kind of spiritual alumnus taking his moral finals', especially during a spiritual crisis in the late forties, when such an exam did not seem so easy. His personal self-*dis*regard was noted by others.

But his will-genius assumed public importance, too. Lewis's friend Austin Farrer, a priest and theologian, has described that will in action. Lewis was always ready to rush to the foremost trench, but 'there are frontiersmen and frontiersmen, of course. There is...the Munich school, who will always sell the pass....The typical apologist is a man whose every dyke is his last ditch. He will carry the war into the enemy's country; he will not yield an inch of his own.' About his devotion to people Farrer would go on to say, 'he gave without stint...he really was a Christian—by which I mean, he never thought he had the right to stop'.

Lewis's will worked socially, too. An aspect of his writing and speaking that was also a feature of his character was his argumentativeness (an offshoot of his inherited and, owing to his father, nurtured articulacy). Roger Lancelyn Green reports that an evening with Lewis could be exhilarating but 'exhausting'. His former student, friend, and noted scholar John Lawlor told me that argument was Lewis's fallback position and that he could *seem* arrogant—but welcomed being proven wrong. Yet Jocelyn Gibb, Lewis's friend and editor, says he was never unkind and would adjust his weaponry to the abilities of his company, but 'woe betide you if you made a woolly remark....He would be on you in a flash.' Perhaps Barfield described this aspect of Lewis's character best. 'His skill in dialectical obstetrics was greatly furthered by a characteristic...a certain delight in expounding the obvious and in expounding it meticulously and more than once.' In short, argument for Lewis was recreational or, perhaps better, re-creational.

And how *not* re-creational? Warren describes what would occur at a meeting of the Inklings—that unofficial, highly influential band of friends who met regularly to converse, smoke, read aloud their works-in-progress, and down their pints—if no one had anything to read. 'On these occasions the fun would be riotous, with Jack at the top of his form...an outpouring of wit, nonsense, whimsy, dialectical swordplay...as I have rarely seen equaled.' Surely he would have agreed with the English philosopher Michael Oakeshott (1901–90) who, in 'The Voice of Poetry in the Conversation of Mankind', tells us that in conversation, 'thoughts of different species take wing...nobody asks where they have come from or on what authority they are present....There is no symposiarch or arbiter.' He concludes this passage with a piece of wisdom that surely Lewis understood. 'Conversation is not an enterprise designed to yield an extrinsic profit....it is an unrehearsed intellectual adventure. It is with conversation as it is with gambling, its significance lies...in wagering.'

According to Kenneth Tynan, the producer, director, and critic (and Lewis's student), Lewis was reminiscent of Samuel Johnson, the towering 18th-century figure whose conversation was made legendary by James Boswell, his contemporaneous biographer. John Wain (Lewis's student, poet, biographer, and future Professor of Poetry at Oxford University) would call him 'a dramatic personality' who 'treated life as if it were an art....always giving a performance and inviting the audience to collaborate....Such people are in fact...out to get, and to give, as much fun as possible.'

His reading habits were as vital and as intense as his conversation. Pencil or pen in hand, he would annotate the margins of almost every book he read, underlining along the way. Sometimes he would write as much on a page as was printed. Often he would add a headnote on each page summarizing its contents, so that a running summary of the entire book emerged. Sometimes, if there were no index, he would provide one. Walter Hooper, for a few weeks Lewis's last secretary, has recounted a revealing exchange between himself and the great literary critic and theorist I. A. Richards, with whom (to say the least) Lewis disagreed. Hooper showed Richards Lewis's copy of Richards's own landmark, *The Principles of Literary Criticism*. After reading Lewis's notes, Richards lamented that had he seen them before he finished the book 'it would have been a much better book'.

'Behind enemy lines'

Lewis was indeed very much his own man. In that light, his radical treatment of culture per se enters our portrait. Note him (cheekiness, again) nearly trivializing (is that too strong a word?) an existential threat to Western culture in 'Learning in War-time', a sermon preached at the University Church of St Mary the Virgin on 22 October 1939:

> The war creates no absolutely new situation: it simply aggravates the permanent human situation so that we can no longer ignore it.... Human culture has always had to exist under the shadow of something infinitely more important than itself.... I reject at once an idea...that cultural activities are in their own right spiritual and meritorious.

As we shall see, two years later, in the now-classic *The Screwtape Letters*, diabolical Uncle Screwtape would confirm this very perspective to his pathetic nephew Wormwood.

More to the point is 'Christianity and Literature' (also 1939). There Lewis argues that a striking *contrast* exists between the basic principles of modern literary criticism and those of the New Testament: 'creative', 'spontaneous', and 'freedom' rule the former; whereas 'convention', 'rules', and 'discipleship' inform the latter—not an argument against culture per se, but certainly the sort of scepticism that breaks ranks. In 'Christianity and Culture' (1940) Lewis goes farther still by questioning the uses of culture. He finds that the strictly natural level of creation, including culture, is bound within a Christian, supernatural perspective, and that the New Testament is 'decidedly cold to culture', warning, as it does, against any kind of superiority. (Lewis frequently reverses our habitual perspective.)

He reminds us that 'good taste' is not a spiritual value and concludes that, though culture-sellers (like Lewis himself, he says) may include Christians, they should serve mostly as an antidote to the age! Finally, there is 'On Living in an Atomic Age' (1948). Such an age, Lewis tells us, is no different than 'an age of Viking raids, plague, or death-by-auto accident'. He says, 'such threats may break our bodies (microbes can do that) but they need not dominate our minds'.

After all, everything (including all civilizations) will end in oblivion, and their durations will have been infinitesimal compared to the 'oceans of dead time' both before and after. Here is a characteristic, and unsparing, Lewisian reversal:

> We must resolutely train ourselves that survival of man on this earth...must be only by honorable and merciful means....Those who care for something else more than civilization are the only people by whom civilization is likely to be preserved.

In short, Lewis was certainly counter-cultural; that is, he ran counter to his own culture and to culture generally when idolized (an admonition we see both in *The Screwtape Letters* and in the second half of *Mere Christianity*).

Surely Lewis's sharp-shooter's application of the phrase 'enemy-occupied territory' to Western culture must come to mind. And yet, notwithstanding his severe stance—in 'Lilies that Fester' (1955) he urges 'rebellion', claiming 'there is no time to spare'—he was not like the terrible prophet Jeremiah crying in the wilderness. There was simply too much merriment, vitality, and hope in the man.

Reputation

In his *C. S. Lewis: Apostle to the Skeptics*, the first study of Lewis's work (1949) and a template still very much worth reading, Chad Walsh makes Lewis's wholeness clear, and his title is perfect; Lewis is the apostle to sceptics, not necessarily atheists. Also well worth reading (for their first-hand accounts of Lewis) are Roger Lancelyn Green's *C. S. Lewis* (1963), Jocelyn Gibb's edited work *Light on C. S. Lewis* (1965, nine essays that evidence the breadth of Lewis's work and personality), *C. S. Lewis at the Breakfast Table* (1979, a collection of essays mostly by those who knew him early and late), Carolyn Keefe's authoritative *C. S. Lewis: Speaker and Teacher* (1971), Stephen Schofield's *In Search of C. S. Lewis* (1983), and John Lawlor's beautifully written *C. S. Lewis: Memories and Reflections* (1998).

The many voices in these books (before, shortly after, and a generation beyond Lewis's death) demonstrate a continuity of interest in the man and the contours of his reputation (as has the proliferation of Screwtape-type letters written by others, my personal favourite being Richard Platt's *As One Devil to Another*, 2012). None of these books is dated, all remain evergreen.

One surprising article on Lewis that stands out came fifty years ago and is largely unnoticed in Lewis commentary. In May of 1959 'Christian Spaceman—C. S. Lewis', by the influential critic and book reviewer Edmund Fuller, appeared in the highbrow, culturally eclectic hardcover magazine *Horizon*, an event, for its length and analytical richness but also for its prophetic insights. For example, in introducing Americans to the Space Trilogy (1938, 1943, 1945) Fuller makes the following tangential observation, so utterly surprising to us more than fifty years later:

> I rate high among Lewis's accomplishments a work *generally less well known* [my emphasis; this is 1959 remember], as yet, than the trilogy but for which I predict a growing reputation and a long life. This is the series of seven books for children which compose *The Chronicles of Narnia*.

He then gives a wonderfully inviting interpretation of *The Chronicles*. But he ends his essay with an appreciation: 'I am grateful to Lewis for some of my richest experiences of mind and heart', leaving us with choice imagery from Deep Heaven (*not* Narnia) and writing, 'am I to say these are not real? I count [those books] among the great symbolic visions of ultimate reality which reveal to us that we are more...than the data our senses can record'.

On the other hand, twenty years ago Christopher Hewetson, the vicar of what for three decades had been C. S. Lewis's church in Headington Quarry, Oxford, seemed to sum up the English attitude towards the great man perfectly. He told his congregation that, yes, perhaps the time had come to improve their 'connection with C.S. Lewis'. After all, Mr Hewetson continued, 'when I came here three and a half years ago...[t]here was a certain "yes but". I found it difficult to get a well-known preacher to preach at the dedication of the Narnia window. *Since then his rating has increased* [my emphasis].... He was a very committed Christian.... We must be proud of our connection with him.'

But this good man was wrong. By the time of the vicar's condescension, Lewis had already been the most famous Christian apologist writing in English.

That reminds me of a visit made to Lewis by Bob Jones, Jr, the Christian Fundamentalist preacher and academic from Bob Jones University. He would check for himself on this very popular, presumably Christian, apologist. He did have reservations, but at the end of the day, he opined, 'that man smokes a pipe, and that man drinks liquor—but I do believe he is a Christian!'

Thirty years ago (fifteen after Jones's visit), the *New York Times* offered 'C. S. Lewis, Gone But Hardly Forgotten', by Michael Nelson, not at all condescending, except towards J. B. Phillips who in 1967 reported that Lewis, as 'ruddy' (as opposed to ghostly) as ever, had appeared twice to him in his sitting room and given Phillips a piece of personal, much-needed advice. Decades later the saintly Rowan Williams writes *The Lion's World* and gets much wrong, as Tom Shippey pointed out in his *Times Literary Supplement* review. (One mistake: Susan could not return to Narnia, *not* because she began to wear lipstick but because she denied Narnia, where she had been a queen.)

A fugitive C. S. Lewis

Was Lewis essentially a fugitive, from culture, from the spirit of his age, perhaps from time itself? I believe he was. In his second published work, a narrative poem called *Dymer* (1926; Lewis was still years away from theism, let alone Christianity), the eponymous hero rebels against the Perfect City, dying as a result. This escape motif irrupted consistently, beginning with his *first* published book, a cycle of poems called *Spirits in Bondage* (1919; Lewis was twenty years old: the title says it all). There, in 'Dungeon Gates', the speaker tells us that 'Our vision still, one moment was enough, | We know we are not made of mortal stuff. . . . For we have seen the Glory—we have seen.' The motif runs to the last paragraph Lewis saw through the press in *Letters to Malcolm, Chiefly on Prayer*.

This is the Lewis template. No wonder in 'The Prudent Jailer' (1947) he has the prisoner say, 'Escapists? Yes. Looking at bars | And chains, we think of files', only to have the jailer say, 'The proper study of prisoners | Is prison.' But the prisoner—one of the few 'whose faith is whole'—has the last word: 'Stone walls cannot a prison make | Half so secure as rigmarole.' We will see it starkly in *The Pilgrim's Regress: An Allegorical Apology for Christianity, Reason, and Romanticism*, with its double helix of escape and Joy—the call from Heaven itself—expressed in fully Christian terms for the first time.

Not surprisingly, many people have noted something opaque about Lewis, opaque even to himself—he admits as much in his autobiography, *Surprised by Joy* (1955)—and we know that as a young man he had his secrets, not least those held from his father. I believe there was a part of him that, like the rest of us, he had to discover as his life unfolded. We certainly know that under certain circumstances he favoured indirection. Perhaps, too, the charismatic public persona covered an interior mystic (which he would have denied but which some of the poetry and parts of the fictions affirm). Keats is right. There was just more there in Lewis: more intellect, imagination, will, energy (mental and physical), devotion, personality (with all its good cheer, humour, argumentativeness, and generosity), as well as more complexity than in most people.

More specifically, I believe Lewis's achievement lies in the following: (1) his personal influence upon very many millions of people is deep, significant, and abiding; (2) his personality and life continue to arouse interest; (3) his many voices have produced a trenchant body of work that includes hallmarks of its many types, remains relevant, and invites commentary; and, especially in that light, (4) as a prose stylist his gifts of wit, analogy, imagery, epigrammatic economy, rhythmical dexterity, and rhetorical adroitness should place him in any canon worthy of study by anyone who pretends to know—let alone to teach—the literature of English-speaking peoples.

Chapter 2
Roots

In his autobiography Lewis calls his upbringing 'nominally Christian'. Though not, I think, a deliberate misdirection, it seems to fit a self-image: there was not much to hold him back from the atheism that eventually crept in. But looking at Lewis's family we must ask, how 'nominal'?

The happy beginning

In fact the boy's character was forged within a closely knit Christian family that worshipped, prayed, observed the pieties, and (on his mother's side) were descended from clergymen, some of noteworthy rank. Lewis's father, Albert (1863–1929), whose forebears were Welsh boilermakers and shipbuilders, pursued Flora Hamilton (1862–1908) for many years. He had first proposed in 1886, the year after he got his solicitor's licence; they finally married in 1894. A sometimes overbearing and always garrulous and argumentative man, Albert became a successful lawyer and a local public figure of some repute. (Ironically, he would admonish Jacksie not to talk too much.) Flora, the beating heart of the household, was an educated woman, 'a voracious reader of good novels' (according to Lewis) who had published a short story, witnessed a miracle when the preserved body of a saint opened her eyes and stared into Flora's own, and had won university honours in logic and mathematics. The two were devoted to each other, though Flora thought Albert too gloomy.

Warren ('Warnie' to family and friends, eventually 'the Major') came upon the scene in 1895 (d. 1973); three years later, on 29 November 1898, Clive Staples was born. The brothers would become and remain the closest of friends. In fact, spiritual intimations (but only that) would first come to Lewis in his very early childhood by way of a toy garden that Warnie had made within the lid of a biscuit tin. That bed of moss embroidered with twigs and flowers taught Lewis beauty and made him aware of nature as something 'dewy, fresh, exuberant', even more than the real garden. 'As long as I live,' he would write, 'my imagination of Paradise will retain something of my brother's toy garden.'

Young Jacksie came to relish the Irish countryside, especially the Castlereagh Hills, those 'Green Hills' so remote from the actual landscape, 'to a child quite unattainable' he would write. 'They taught me longing—*Sehnsucht*', that sharp pang of sweet desire that calls from beyond the world, perhaps calling us home. This 'Joy', as Lewis would call it (a 'technical term'), would become the centre of Lewis's spiritual life, of his conversion, and, later, of his apologetic project.

Much that he writes will either discuss or seek to convey Joy: the early poem 'Joy', the later poem 'The Day with a White Mark' ('who knows if it will ever come again...when sudden heaven in man begins or ends'), *The Pilgrim's Regress* (especially in the Preface to the third edition, where he corrects his too-loose use of 'Romanticism'), his great and defining sermon 'The Weight of Glory', and, of course, the autobiography proper, *Surprised by Joy*, its title taken from a poem by William Wordsworth.

In 1905, with Albert prospering, the family moved into a large house, 'Little Lea', in County Down, one with many corridors and rooms far removed from the main living space. There the boy had the run of his father's considerable library and would read compulsively. Eventually he would use the house in both *The Lion, the Witch and the Wardrobe* and *The Magician's Nephew*, the first and the sixth books of *The Chronicles of Narnia*. (My numbering accords with the order of composition, the order in which they should be read.) And the Northern Irish landscape *is* Narnia: I have never seen such green nor felt such freshness. His greatest recreation largely springs from his own imagination. He would begin writing early in the Little End Room (as he came to call it), a refuge secluded from the rest of the house by those long corridors (see Figure 2).

This happy life would come to include the governess, Annie Harper, cousins, aunts, and uncles, and a lifelong friend, Arthur Greeves (1895–1966), who lived nearby and shared with Lewis a deep love for Norse mythology, Lewis's favourite and yet another source of Joy. 'Balder the beautiful'—the god Odin's son—'is dead,

2. The Lewis family, 'Jacksie' far right in Flora's lap, seated in front of Albert.

is dead', is a line that would haunt Lewis. The two would visit and correspond their whole lives, in adolescence writing frankly about sex.

Especially memorable were trips (for example to London, where Jacksie was enthralled by live mice, and to the south of France) with Flora and Warnie, but not with Albert, who did not like leaving home. And in the Little End Room he would write a collection of stories about dressed and talking animals, a portentous achievement.

Boxen

An oddity of Lewis's early life (Walter Hooper places him at about the age of seven, perhaps eight) is not that the boy would attempt to write stories; given his pedigree and precocity that makes perfect sense. What surprises is that they would be both rich in their details of character, plot, and social convention and yet so imaginatively uninspired. As he would write, they have 'nothing whatever in common with Narnia, except the anthropomorphic beasts'. He continues, 'Animal-Land, by its whole quality, *excluded the least hint of wonder* [my emphasis]'.

Nevertheless, the whole is revealing. It combines Animal-Land and 'India', Warren's contribution. Jacksie had already written up stories with a medieval setting (surely another foreshadowing of interests to come); then, when Warnie was home on vacation, he added present-day tales. These were joined with India. The countries were separated by water, but Warnie worked out steamship routes between the two. Along the way a reader encounters maps, tables, and several pictures (many in colour) drawn by Jacksie to scale, with cross-hatching, correct perspectives, and characters properly dressed.

The stories range in length from whole tales to 'novels', thirteen in all. The collection in *Boxen: The Imaginary World of the*

Young C. S. Lewis (1985) contains the thirteen stories (the first being a three-act play, perfectly formatted and including stage directions) and Lewis's own 'Encyclopedia Boxoniana', written when he visited Little Lea in 1927–8: an inventory of stories and fragments and a Chronology stretching from the 11th century to 1909.

Among the many characters is Littlemaster, a position occupied by Lord Big, a frog who (Lewis allowed) might remind one of Albert (known to the brothers as 'Pudaita-bird'). Regions are named and described. Psychology, rhetoric, politics, and battles all make appearances, as does the Viscount Puddiphat, an owl who owns music halls. (A different owl would make an important appearance in *Prince Caspian*, the second of *The Chronicles*.) Consider this snippet from 'A History of Mouse-Land from Stone-Age to Bubblish I (Old History)':

> The new chief of the Cosy tribe was named after his country: 'bubblish'. ... When he got there he found that they had chosen another Mouse to be king named Poplar. Bublish pretendit [*sic*] to be quite loyal to him but made him promise that after his death Bublish schould [*sic*] rule.

All seems to be a distillation of their reading and of conversations the boys overheard, for their father and his cronies would talk, preach, rant, and debate politics over and again—often requiring the boys' presence. But in the stories Lewis's attention to conflict, suspense, and motivation is palpable. The work can be best thought of, I think, both as a training-ground and a sowing of seed (see Figure 3).

His earliest letters are to his pet mouse, Tommy, surely a forerunner of 'the gay and martial' Reepicheep from *The Chronicles*. He pays much attention to animals and writes to Warnie about them, as he does about Boxen. 'At present Boxen is *slightly* convulsed,' he writes in 1906, 'the news has just reached her that King Bunny is a prisoner.' Other letters, however, bode ill.

3. The front cover of *Boxen*.

In May of 1908 he writes to Warnie, 'mamy is doing well indeed', though she would soon be mortally ill. And on 29 September of that same year (a month after Flora's catastrophic death), with Albert already having sent Jacksie to join Warren at Wynyard School, he writes, 'Mr. Capron [the headmaster] said some-thing [*sic*] I am not [likely] to forget, "curse the boy" (behind Warnie's back)...We simply *cannot* wait in this hole until the end of term.' Warren was writing similarly. Capron would soon become overtly sadistic and finally be certified insane.

So Jacksie would be attentive, quick, and smart, as well as extremely literate and desirous of being left alone when he so chose; and he would be wilful. The household also included a bigoted nanny, volubly anti-Catholic beyond conventional norms. At some depth Lewis would harbour that prejudice his whole life.

Misery and more

His atheism surely has its roots in Flora's death from cancer on 23 August 1908, after a long, horrific struggle. That was Albert's forty-fifth birthday (his own father had died earlier that year). Jacksie was not quite ten. 'The great continent had sunk like Atlantis', Lewis would write. Research tells us that such a loss has far-reaching consequences, but his few and brief references to it imply that it did not hold any spiritual significance for him: he would attribute his atheism to other causes but never to his crushing despair at having prayed futilely to a 'magician god' as Flora lay dying. Much later, in *The Magician's Nephew*, he would movingly describe a scene of a dying mother magically recovering owing to the bravery of her obedient son. In the event, Flora's death marks the end of the first, foundational, stage of Lewis's character-formation.

Eventually Albert removed Lewis from the schools he hated (including one that Warren thought highly of) and sent him to Surrey to a private tutor, William T. Kirkpatrick, 'The Great Knock', an atheist who had tutored both Albert and Warren. To the rhetorical and argumentative disposition Lewis inherited from Albert, Kirkpatrick added dialectical precision: everything would be expressed accurately, defined, and defended rationally. Lewis blossomed. He came to love this man who had no small talk and

The left margin has "C. S. Lewis" rotated.

argued relentlessly, taught him classical languages and literature, prepared him for Oxford, and allowed him to read wantonly.

One book would change him forever, George MacDonald's *Phantastes*, which he read on 4 March 1916. The hero, Anodos ('pathless'), enters fairy land in pursuit of his ideal of the feminine, the Marble Lady. The landscape and creatures, as well as a palace where Anodos stays for a long spell (and which he later finds is his), become ever more enchanting, not least when encountering Cosmo's story about his attempt to free his lover from a mirror. Hyper-reality has replaced the real world, a hyper-reality marked by holiness. 'That night my imagination was, in a certain sense, baptized', Lewis wrote, 'the rest of me not unnaturally took longer. I had not the faintest notion what I had let myself in for by buying *Phantastes*.'

As thoroughly as Kirkpatrick had prepared Lewis for entrance into Oxford, it was not thoroughly enough. Lewis failed responsions, not because of its Latin and Greek components but because of its basic algebra requirement, and would never have entered the university had he not volunteered for service in World War I. (As an Irishman he was exempt from the draft.) In the event he won a scholarship to University College and very soon found himself billeted at Keble College with Paddy Moore, the son of Janie King Moore (1872–1951). That meeting would change Lewis's life. The two young men made an agreement: if one fell in battle and the other survived, that survivor would care for the dead comrade's family.

Once in the trenches ('this is war; this is what Homer wrote about') he saw his sergeant blown to bits next to him, took prisoners (though under what were regarded as laughable circumstances—the Germans did *not* want to surrender to the French), and was badly wounded by friendly artillery fire. While recovering Lewis begged his father to visit, but Albert, who seemed confused and, remember, hated travelling, did not.

Lewis would be long in forgiving him. In the event Paddy was killed in action. So when Lewis returned from the army he was as good as his word, and a long, complex relationship with Mrs Moore (known as 'Minto') began, including a cohabitation that included Mrs Moore's young daughter, Maureen, and, eventually, a sexual relationship with his mother-surrogate. It took him longer to forgive himself than to forgive Albert.

Spirits in Bondage

All along, in pursuit of his first ambition, Lewis had been writing poetry. His first publication (under the pseudonym Clive Hamilton) is a cycle of poems, *Spirits in Bondage* (1919), in three parts: 'The Prison House', with twenty-one poems; 'Hesitation', with three poems; and 'The Escape', with sixteen poems. The movement is first downward and bitter, then rising, if not quite to hope proper then to hopefulness. Lewis himself wrote that the cycle was 'mainly strung round the idea . . . that nature is wholly diabolical and malevolent and that God, if He exists, is outside of and in opposition to the cosmic arrangement'. That is, 'matter=nature=Satan. And on the other side Beauty, the only spiritual & non-natural thing that I have yet found.' (The descent/ ascent movement would find its way into other Lewis works, such as *Perelandra* and *A Grief Observed*.)

Warren disliked the book, calling Jack's atheism 'academic'. It also troubled Albert, from whom Lewis tried to hide his atheism. The poet is clearly conflicted, and conflicted he would remain, for quite a while. Angry at what he professes to disbelieve, he yet longs to believe in something beyond beauty:

> Too often have I sat alone
> When the wet night falls heavily,
> and fretting winds around me moan,
> And homeless longing vexes me

For lore that I will never know,
And visions none can hope to see,
Till brooding works upon me so
A childish fear steals over me.

Some of this is adolescent posturing, but much of it is based on Lewis's war experience and is utterly authentic, although he was not a 'war poet' and paid as little attention to it as possible, claiming that the many corpses he saw were no surprise: they reminded him of his mother's. It is skilfully wrought verse, which Lewis would compose all his life.

Worthy of note here is a bit of literary history. Around that time Lewis was enjoying John Masefield's poetry, but three years after the publication of *Spirits in Bondage*, T. S. Eliot would bring out *The Waste Land*. If it did not exactly usher in literary Modernism it certainly raised its flag, at least in poetry—though not in Lewis's own. Referring to a very famous line from Eliot's 'The Love Song of J. Alfred Prufrock', he would write that he 'could never see a patient etherized upon a table' when looking at the night sky. Indeed he already was what he called himself in 'De Descriptione Temporum', his inaugural lecture (1954) as the Professor of Medieval and Renaissance English Literature at Cambridge University: a dinosaur, that is, an 'Old Western man'.

Between 1919 and 1923, Lewis and the two Moores lived in eight different homes. The arrangement deeply troubled both Warnie and Albert, whom his son was deceiving; it is the lowest moral point of Lewis's life. Albert knew that his son could be 'cajoled by any woman who has been through the mill'; Warnie called the arrangement 'freakish'. The Little End Room, where the boy could be alone and self-indulgent, had become a secret household.

This may have been an instance of what Lewis's pupil Christopher Derrick called *Weiberherrschaft*, a sort of self-indenturing to women. If so it would apply, as we shall see, to Joy Davidman, whom Lewis married when she was put 'through the mill' suffering terribly from cancer. And it certainly is an example of Farrer's belief that Lewis, as a Christian, thought 'he never had the right to stop'.

In July of 1923 he took his third First ('Mods', or Greek and Latin language and literature, and 'Greats', classical Greek and Roman history and philosophy, had been the first two, followed by English language and literature—doing in three years what should have taken six). He had won the Chancellor's Prize for an English Essay on 'Optimism'. Still he had time to join the Martlets, a literary society where papers were read and criticized, often mercilessly. Lewis was a member from 1919 to 1940, when he read his last paper in which he introduces the conception of 'The Kappa Element in Fiction'; it would become the famous essay 'On Stories'.

After getting his degree Lewis was passed over for many fellowships, finally being asked to deputize for E. F. Carritt as a philosophy tutor during the academic year 1924–5. During that year the atheist lectured on 'The Moral Good—Its Place Among the Values', with special attention to David Hume's *An Enquiry Concerning Human Understanding*, section X, Hume's refutation of the miraculous; twenty years later the Christian would refute Hume in his 1947 book, *Miracles*. (And his thinking about the moral code—he had already written a dissertation on 'The Hegemony of Moral Values'—would enter into many essays and, above all, into his examination of the Natural Law in *The Abolition of Man*, 1943.)

In May he was elected to a fellowship in English at Magdalen College, where he would remain for thirty years. Soon after the appointment he joined the Kolbiters, a group begun by a new friend, J. R. R. Tolkien (a philologist and a Catholic, both of which Lewis reported, half-comically, he was told always to distrust).

The purpose of the group was to translate the major documents of Norse mythology. Lewis found it rough and rewarding, but for him there was no such thing as too much conversation.

His letters get longer (especially those to his father) as his friendships grow into a band of brothers that would endure: Owen Barfield, Hugo Dyson, Neville Coghill, Cecil Harwood, A. K. Hamilton-Jenkin, Colin Hardie. Eventually he would thank his father for all his support, but he would not warm to him until Albert was near death; nor would he repent of his resentment until long after that. All along—with the maintenance of a troubled and troubling household, near-poverty and fraudulence, exhausting academic work, professional worry, society memberships, the writing of lectures and of a narrative poem, as well as prodigious letter-writing—Lewis kept a diary.

All My Road Before Me: The Diary of C. S. Lewis, 1922–1927

Lewis begins the diary at the suggestion of Mrs Moore, who will become his audience. The first entry comes three years after the start of their *ménage*, the final entry four years before he becomes a Christian. He writes nothing of the Inner Life that he would later describe in his autobiography and that will conduce to his conversion; so in that respect he is false to Mrs Moore, about whom he is false to Albert, who takes a lamentable beating throughout. At one point, while accepting a cheque from his father, he complains over Albert's advice that he spend less. And he is false to friends, too. Not only did Albert not know of his arrangement with Mrs Moore but neither did Owen Barfield, who was fast becoming his closest friend after Warren. In fact, Barfield was greatly surprised to learn that in the diary there is no mention of his philosophical 'Great War' with Lewis, a long disputation that *seemed* to have taken up very much of Lewis's intellectual and emotional oxygen.

He records several telling dreams; in one he is the hero during a stabbing, in another he converts an 'aesthete' of a 'Satanic sneer'. He describes the harrowing two weeks spent with Doc, Mrs Moore's brother, who was losing his mind—a foreshadowing, surely, of the Un-man in *Perelandra*—and seriously considers taking the Civil Service exam, tougher, he thinks, than the entrance exam for the university. He describes how he saved Maisie, a young woman who was being abused by her parents, and mentions the pivotally influential Chesterton but not his *The Everlasting Man*, so prominent in the autobiography. MacDonald is hardly mentioned at all. He finds Maureen Moore's First Communion disgusting, her Confirmation like the 'slaughtering of a pig'. He plays games (chess, bridge, badminton) and swims. Sleeping no more than five or six hours a night, he has an enormous, almost preternatural, appetite for work. (Once, when he could not sleep, he rereads Book Two of Plato's *Republic*, necessarily in Greek; it would be important in the epic narrative poem he was writing.)

The great value of his diary is this: it shows us the man Lewis converted *from*, and the reader is relieved to be done with it. The death of Lewis's mother; his resentment of his father who, along with the 'magician god' (as Lewis called him), failed to save Flora; his liaison with Mrs Moore, mother-surrogate and instrument of revenge on his father; and his own summary of *Dymer*, the long poem to come, wherein 'a man . . . on some mysterious bride, begets a monster: which monster, as soon as it has killed its father, becomes a God' (about which summary Lewis would profess, 'of course, I'm not Dymer'): these and much else symptomize a hidden self that Lewis must overcome.

No wonder Warnie characterized his brother's conversion as fundamentally a return to sanity. The last line of the diary reads, 'Is there never to be any peace or comfort?' That from a man who some twenty years later, as a Christian, would write 'We Have No "Right to Happiness"'. First the neo-Pagan; then the Christian convert (see Figure 4).

4. **C. S. Lewis (left), Janie King Moore ('Minto'), and Warren Hamilton Lewis.**

Dymer

Finally *Dymer*, the poem on which Lewis has been working assiduously, is published in 1926 (a second, definitive edition in 1950 arrives in *C. S. Lewis: Narrative Poems*, edited by Walter Hooper). It contains nine cantos, each with more than thirty stanzas in rhyme royal, a seven-line stanza rhyming ababbcc, in iambic pentameter.

The story, which Lewis first attempted in prose, is exciting, mysterious, and convoluted, though Lewis never loses the thread. The eponymous young hero escapes from a totalitarian state (there is Book Two of Plato's *The Republic*); commits a murder; wanders through a lush forest; meets a girl who satisfies his lust; leaves her and when attempting to return is blocked by a hag (the same woman transformed?); learns that he has sparked a revolution; meets a sinister magician who prompts Dymer to dream; learns from one of those dreams that he was in love with his own lust; is shot by the magician; finds his beloved but learns that she is nothing more than his desire for desire itself; meets

27

an angelic guardian who tells of the monster he begat on the unidentified girl; and confronts that son in battle and is killed, that monster-son then becoming a god.

Many critics, including many of Lewis's friends, thought *Dymer* a good poem containing complex ideas and engaging verse. But what matters most is the effect of this poem on Lewis. He was near-obsessing about 'the Christina Dream' adapted from that of Christina Pontifex in Samuel Butler's *The Way of All Flesh*. For Lewis it epitomized all sorts of desire, including both Joy and sexual desire: it was Lewis himself who wrote that he underestimated the difficulty of overcoming lust. *Dymer* exorcized the obsession. Moreover, it catalysed Lewis, now untrusting of introspection, to search outside of himself for sources of Joy.

Perhaps that 'nominally Christian' home had done its work after all. Consider the following, from near the beginning of *Dymer*:

> O! but we shall keep
> Our vision still, One moment was enough,
> We know we are not made of mortal stuff.
> And we can bear all the trials that come after,
> [...]
> For we have seen the Glory—we have seen.

Now this, the very last stanza of the poem:

> And from the distant corner of day's birth
> He heard clear trumpets blowing and bells ring,
> A noise of great good coming into the earth
> And such a music that the dumb would sing
> If Balder had led back the blameless spring
> With victory, with the voice of charging spears,
> And in white lands long-lost Saturnian years.

In some sense we must suppose he was an atheist. But with the weeds now cleared away he seems an unsteady atheist ready for fruitful religious cultivation. Nevertheless, any consideration of Lewis's 'self' is something of a minefield. He hid, distorted, invented, denied, and finally transcended it. Always he coyly warned us against discussing it.

Box 1 The Inklings

The Inklings were an informal group of like-minded men who met regularly to converse and to read aloud works-in-progress. An Inklings group pre-dates the Lewis group, but, when its founder left, Lewis kept the name. The height of the group's vitality extends from the mid-1930s to the mid-1950s, but some elements of the group continued to meet until Lewis's death in 1963. They met regularly, sometimes in college rooms but normally on Tuesday mornings in the Eagle and Child, then on Thursday evenings as well at the Lamb and Flag. The meetings became sufficiently well known so that a novelist could have a character know it was Tuesday by seeing Lewis enter the 'Bird and Baby' (that is, the Eagle and Child): 'there goes C. S. Lewis', says the detective Gervase Fen. Participants varied, of course, over the decades, some dropping in only once or a few times, others dropping out. Some of the regular members (I follow Hooper's *Companion*) were:

C. S. Lewis
Warren Lewis
J. R. R. Tolkien
Owen Barfield, of whom Lewis wrote, 'he towers above us all'
Hugo Dyson, who visited from Reading
Charles Williams, who had moved up from London
Robert Havard (or Humphrey, or the U.Q., for Useless Quack), Lewis's physician
Colin Hardie, a Classics tutor at Magdalen College
Lord David Cecil, a Fellow in History at Wadham College
R. B. McCallum, a Fellow and Tutor in Modern History at Pembroke College
Tom Stevens, an ancient historian and Magdalen College colleague
Charles Wrenn, the Rawlinson and Bosworth Professor of Anglo-Saxon at Oxford

Adam Fox, a colleague at Magdalen College

J. A. W. Bennett, a widely travelled colleague of Lewis's at Magdalen College

James Dundas-Grant, a Navy man resident at Magdalen College

Neville Coghill, one of Lewis's oldest friends and colleagues at the university

Fr. Gervase Mathew, an archaeologist, and 'one of the sweetest men I've ever met'

Christopher Tolkien, J. R. R. Tolkien's son and posthumous editor

John Wain, a Lewis pupil, as well as novelist, biographer, and Professor of Poetry

These meetings mattered for two reasons. The first was the sheer conviviality that they offered. With Lewis at the centre—all agreed on his wit, his learning-worn-lightly, and his gift for precise, insightful, and spontaneous criticism (not to mention those 'dialectical obstetrics' that Barfield noted)—the fun was sure to abound. The second reason was literary. Any writer knows that one must write for an audience, and there was none better suited to what these men wrote than each other. Certainly not all of the members were writers. And here 'member' is a very loose term: they were an 'unelected and undetermined circle of friends', according to Tolkien. But as Diana Pavlac Glyer has shown in *C. S. Lewis and J. R. R. Tolkien as Writers in Community*, mutual commentary influenced what members wrote: in the case of Tolkien, it (especially Lewis's praise) influenced *that* they wrote. By all accounts criticism was *very* candid.

Chapter 3
Lewis ascendant

'This place has surpassed my wildest dreams', he wrote to Albert
upon arriving in Oxford in 1916 to take his entrance exams.
'I have never seen anything so beautiful, especially on the frosty
moonlight nights.'

Oxford life

With its broad streets and narrow lanes, the ancient city offers both
town and gown: smoky traffic (though not much in Lewis's younger
days), long bus queues, assorted shops, and then the colleges: on the
outside spires rising among the night stars, inside the disappearance
of the 21st century. Magdalen College, Lewis's academic home for
nearly thirty years, enchants with its Deer Park and Addison's Walk.
In plain Mansfield College is the chapel where Lewis preached
'Transposition'. Outside the colleges are the University Church
of St Mary the Virgin, where a multitude heard 'Learning in
War-Time' and 'The Weight of Glory'; Williams Hairdresser on
36 High Street where Lewis thought to write 'The Efficacy of
Prayer'; and both the Eagle and Child ('The Bird and Baby')
and Lamb and Flag, where the Inklings would meet (see Box 1).

Lewis was elected to his fellowship at Magdalen College in 1925;
in 1926 the Lewis men spend their last vacation together, an ill
Albert dying in 1929 two days after Lewis left him to return to

Oxford. While in Ireland in 1930 to close up affairs, Warren begins his monumental task of editing the Lewis Family Papers, so important to understanding his brother's life. Also in 1930, Jack, Warren, and Mrs Moore buy the Kilns, where the brothers would live for the rest of Lewis's life. By the middle of 1931 Jack and Warnie (still in the army) quite separately find their way back to Christianity. After a posting in Shanghai, Warnie (a captain) retires and takes up residence in the Kilns. Though many visitors find Mrs Moore kind, Warnie does not warm to her; few people will learn that she is not the brothers' actual mother. Mrs Moore, thinking Lewis 'as good as having another servant', interrupts him peremptorily to do chores no matter his work at hand.

He is always writing (when not talking, that is), with letters abounding. (He is probably writing *The Queen of Drum*, a narrative poem, around this time.) His most frequent correspondent in 1933 is Arthur, to whom, for example, he writes in 1933 that Hitler, owing to his persecution of the Jews and the nonsense he says about them, 'is as contemptible for his stupidity as he is detestable for his cruelty'. During this period he engages in that 'Great War' with Owen Barfield, mostly about imagination but also about language (especially metaphor) and Anthroposophy, the philosophy of Rudolph Steiner (he of the Waldorf Schools). Lewis finally comes to see it, with its mysticism and occultism, as a version of the Gnostic heresy, and would lose interest in the 'war' after his conversion.

With this we see the start of a pattern. Alan Griffiths was a student and became a friend; then he became a Catholic: Dom Bede Griffiths, OSB, who would start an ashram in India and there be revered. He and Lewis corresponded about Catholicism and Protestantism until Lewis cut off that topic; rarely would he revisit it in any form with anyone. And, most tellingly, he lost interest in Joy itself after his conversion. Noteworthy in this respect are the number of times in his fiction—in the Underworld of

33

The Silver Chair, at the end of *Till We Have Faces*, most notably during the debate in *Perelandra*—that speech is abruptly terminated, either by violence or death.

And there was the prank. Adam Fox, one of Lewis's breakfast companions, an Inkling and a minor poet, thought the newly elected Professor of Poetry (E. K. Chambers) was undeserving, so Lewis and Tolkien successfully campaigned to have Fox elected. Some years later, when Lewis was a candidate, he narrowly lost to C. Day-Lewis. It's not nice to fool *alma mater*.

A Christian, and an apologist

The decade nearly begins with *The Pilgrim's Regress* (1933), an allegory written immediately after his conversion and encompassing virtually the whole of the intellectual spirit of his age, most of it now in ruins. It is a template of Lewis's apologetic thinking. (His use here of his own experience becomes a recurring feature of his work.) Thereafter, though, his professional achievements make his reputation: *The Allegory of Love*, a prize-winning landmark of literary history (1936); *The Personal Heresy* (1939); and *Rehabilitations* (1939), a collection of literary essays.

Near the end of the decade he writes *Out of the Silent Planet* (1938, which, along with *Perelandra* and *That Hideous Strength*, the second and third books of the Space Trilogy, we discuss in Chapter 4), delivers 'Learning in War-Time' (1939), and soon is invited by Ashley Sampson, editor of the Christian Challenge series, to write *The Problem of Pain* (1940). Thus do we witness the start of Lewis's professional life book-ended by his apologetic emergence.

Surprised by Joy, the Shape of My Early Life

Learning from Lewis of his conversion at the start of the decade must begin with *Surprised by Joy, the Shape of My Early Life*

(1956), even though it is written some twenty years after the fact, when he is already famous.

What Lewis calls 'the dialectic of desire' is essentially a process of trial and error as one seeks the source of Joy: Culture? Sex? Familial love or friendship? and the like. Religious belief had peeked through in his early poetry, but Chesterton's *Everlasting Man* unsettles him, just as spiritual sentiment had been stirred by *Phantastes* when he was sixteen ('an atheist cannot be too careful of his reading'). Lewis writes of his official self—the atheist, diligent undergraduate, dutiful tutor—and of his deeper, or hidden, self, the one who was nourished by the 'wrong' books (Chesterton, MacDonald).

He writes of his family, boyhood, schooling, and friends. He recounts his enthralment with myth, especially Norse myth. He does *not* write about the fraudulent, secret self. (Mrs Moore is not mentioned, though a 'long, complex episode' is, barely.) Along the way he guides his reader through intellectual stages (from strict materialism—atoms are all—to Berkley's Subjective Idealism, that tells us the world is fundamentally mental; that is, of God's mind), and he describes his self-examination: why do the books I disagree with move me so deeply? Why does some poetry (e.g. Wordsworth's *The Prelude*) seem to beckon?

In 'Shelley, Dryden, and Mr. Eliot' (1939), Lewis had characterized the concept of myth: '[it] is thus like manna', he writes, 'it is to each man a different dish and to each the dish he needs. It does not grow old nor stick at frontiers...and even from the same man at the same moment it can elicit different responses at different levels.' But in recalling a conversation from 1926, he epitomized his understanding of it: 'The hardest boiled of all the atheists I ever knew', he writes, 'said, "All that [anthropological] stuff...about the Dying God [especially in Sir James George Frazer's *The Golden Bough*]. Rum thing. It almost looks as if it had really happened once."' That is, the shape of the story—a god coming down among us, dying, then rising again—had a resonant allure. Even Lewis, when he encountered it in non-Christian mythologies, found the myth appealing.

Then, years later, on 19 September 1931, there occurred a fateful and historic conversation very late at night. After dinner Hugo Dyson, Tolkien, and Lewis were talking of metaphor, myth, and resurrection as they strolled down Addison's Walk. They were 'interrupted by a rush of wind which came so suddenly', he wrote to Arthur. 'We all held our breath, the other two appreciating the ecstasy of such a thing almost as you would.' That bad weather drove them indoors. Tolkien would leave at 3.00 a.m., Dyson at 4.00 a.m.

To Greeves he wrote, 'I have just passed on from believing in God to definitely believing in Christ.... My long late night talk with Dyson and Tolkien had a great deal to do with it.' The conversation taught Lewis that something which is a *myth* can also be a *fact*, such as the Incarnation, Crucifixion, and Resurrection of Christ. 'If ever a myth had become fact', he writes, '[a god] had been incarnated, it would be just like this.' A great reconciliation had happened. Once he accepted Christ he ceased to be interested in Joy: 'I know that the experience, *considered as a state of my own mind* [my emphasis], had never had the kind of importance I once gave it.' (For this he partially credits Samuel Alexander's *Space, Time, and Deity*, 1920, which teaches the difference between Enjoyment, being inside an experience, and contemplation, examining it from the outside.)

Belief is like diving into water, he wrote; one does not *do* something; rather one *stops* doing something. When he entered, albeit 'kicking, struggling', he found that 'the hardness of God is kinder than the softness of men, His compassion our liberation'. But the appeal is also oxymoronic. On 25 October 1934, he wrote to the critic Paul Elmer More, 'Is the Christian belief not precisely this; that the same being which is eternally...at the End...yet also, in some incomprehensible way, [is a] purposing, feeling, and finally crucified Man in a particular place and time? So that somehow or other, we have it both ways?'

The Pilgrim's Regress

The literary result of Lewis's conversion arrives two years later. In two weeks while in Ireland Lewis writes *Pilgrim's Regress* (1933), a dream-vision about John who (though he doesn't know it) after leaving his home must return. It is his first book that is *not* poetry and *is* Christian. It is nothing less than an announcement: a dynamic new voice backed by a steel-trap mind and an imagination to match has arrived. To be sure, much of the action is intellectual and spiritual, but it is played out by figures who *embody* threats and populate the landscape: that is, allegorical figures. Moreover, something of the utmost consequence is at stake, namely, the hero's spiritual awakening and therefore his soul. Finally, there are physical challenges that would daunt the hardiest reader, with close calls, timely interventions, impossible tasks, and a *denouement* no one would guess but, like all good resolutions, seems probable and is satisfying.

The complexity of the plot is reflected in the detailed and tightly outlined table of contents listing ten Books, each with several chapters. This will not be an easy read. Frightened by the departure of his Uncle George to the island beyond the sea (the 'Landlord' has 'foreclosed') and also of being thrown into the Black Hole, John nevertheless intensely longs to visit the island. He leaves the Landlord's house (and its Stewards) and travels a road fraught with carnality and every –ism fashionably ascendant at the time (Fascism, Communism, Modernism, high church Anglicanism, Hedonism, and more, along with characters representing T. S. Eliot, Irving Babbitt, and Freud). Each either tempts or threatens him. He meets Mr Enlightenment, Mr Sensible, and a hermit named History. After travelling south to the city of Thrill and north to Acropolis, he finally meets Mother Kirk ('church').

From her rocking chair, she tells him to remove his ragged clothes and that the only way home is down the cliff and through a harrowing tunnel that will bring him to a river, which he must swim. Moreover, there is no other source of reliable instruction, no way except through her. As he descends he is terrified, until he hears a trustworthy voice; when he see the man behind that voice he comes to understand the true meaning of myth. The Man says,

> Child, if you will, it is mythology. It is but truth, not fact: an image, not the very real. But then it is My mythology. The words of Wisdom are also myth and metaphor.... But this is My inventing, this is the veil under which I have chosen to appear even from the first until now. For this end I made your senses and for this end your imagination, that you might see My Face and live.

He finds his way back home by way of the same path, now not at all menacing, finally ending where he began. He discovers that he had mistaken distant hills for an island. He learns that the Landlord is good, not least in having sent images to those who need them most. '"We have come back to Puritania," John says to his faithful guide Virtue, '"and that was my father's house."...The shadows lengthened as they went down towards the brook.'

Each page has a running head note summarizing that page. At the beginning of chapter 3 of Book Nine we read, 'He sees the face of Death and learns that dying is the only escape from it.' On that page we learn of a decision, a free choice like the kind Lewis made while on a bus or in a motorcycle sidecar. He hears, 'to you I am not Nothing; I am the being blind-folded...the surrender...the step into the dark...utter helplessness turned out to utter risk: the final loss of liberty'. Mother Kirk had told him he came a long way but that she could have carried him here easily. Or, as Chesterton put it in *The Everlasting Man*, 'there are two ways of getting home; and one of them is to stay there. The other is to walk around the whole world till we come back to the same place.'

C. S. Lewis

In fact, this book is so rich, so taut, and so formidably polemical that, in the 1950 edition, Lewis himself would describe it as 'of uncharitable temper'. I disagree; it is a masterpiece that became his rhetorical template, and it was well received. Owing to the figure of Mother Kirk, its severe orthodoxy (a staple of Lewis's religious writing), and because it was published by Sheed and Ward (a Catholic publisher) people thought he must be a Catholic.

The scholar as celebrity

As a fellow Lewis is tutoring and lecturing. He worked at the latter and became so effective that students packed the hall to hear him (unlike Tolkien, who was known to lecture to one person). Barfield recalls hearing his lecture on 'The Literary Impact of the Authorized Version' at the University of London: 3,000 people, one hour, no manuscript. As a tutor, however, his reviews were mixed. His own standards being so high, he was demanding. Most of his pupils (like Kenneth Tynan, who came to view him as a father figure) found their encounters with him bracing; others, like John Betjeman (later Poet Laureate), came to dislike him intensely. None ever reported that Lewis's own religious beliefs or his vocation as a Christian apologist ever entered into his teaching.

By most accounts his conversation was scintillating. Owen Barfield has emphasized Lewis's humour, the sheer quickness of his mind and expression, and his ability to adjust to different levels of understanding. (He cites a letter that Lewis dashed off of such piquancy and wit that Barfield, no slouch, admits it would have taken him hours to write.) Once, when a dinner companion praised the prospect of 'splicing the glands of young apes onto old gentlemen', Lewis responded, 'I'd rather be an old man than a young monkey'. He did not speak quickly but rather evenly and fluently. In the event Barfield, like so many others, enjoyed 'the abiding flow of his imperturbably analytical judgements as . . . resembling a flood of clear and steady moonlight, settling downward from above and pouring tranquilly over the nooks and crannies of a conversational landscape'.

We have already seen that a good many books influenced Lewis respecting his formation, methods, and ideas. Of particular importance is Richard Hooker's *Laws of Ecclesiastical Politie* (1594, 1597), which taught Lewis a good deal about theology, of course, but also about effective apologetic method. However, two books that mattered are largely overlooked, Edwin Bevan's *Symbolism and Belief* (1938) and, especially, Rudolph Otto's *The Idea of the Holy* (1923).

Bevan seems to have influenced Lewis's indirect, or 'oblique', works (such as *The Chronicles*), advising the writer to avoid 'the direct frontal approach' to God. Otto is theologically the more compelling of the two. In examining holiness he treats certain mysteries, including the *numinous*, that fathomless mystery attaching to the sacred being and the deep enchantment of the worshipper as he contemplates that being. Otto summarizes his belief that 'the holy' is 'an *a priori* category of mind'. That is, it is built into us and so allows us to achieve 'fellowship with "the holy" in knowing, feeling, and willing'. He concludes, 'such a one [with whom we come to know, feel, and will] is more than Prophet. He is the Son.'

During this decade of teaching, talking, reading, and walking, Lewis is also, of course, writing. In the *Collected Letters*, the 1930s run to 315 pages; the longest are to Warnie and Arthur. Poems, too, come forth: sixteen are included in *The Pilgrim's Regress*, another sixteen stand alone (according to Don W. King's magisterial *C. S. Lewis, Poet*). In his bibliography Hooper lists sixteen different sermons and essays published between 1931 and 1940, two of which would be collected in his debate with E. M. W. Tillyard, *The Personal Heresy* and one other included in *Rehabilitations* (1939, again), a collection of nine essays, eight of which were apparently written for that book. That is a total of twenty-four essays (or sermons). Then we have four *other* books.

The Personal Heresy and *Rehabilitations*

The first of these two books consists of a series of exchanges between Lewis and E. M. W. Tillyard, the senior of the two. Lewis objects to the inclusion of the poet's life or intention ('poet' in this case meaning the maker of the poem or story) in any judgement of the work ('postulator', he calls it). But what really sets him off is the notion that somehow 'personality' matters to our judgement. This is more than a hobbyhorse; some years later Lewis will refer to the 'pestilent notion of personality' as a moral danger. He adduces Herrick's poem 'Upon Julia's Clothes': 'Then, then (methinks) how sweetly flows | The liquefaction of her clothes.' If we *contemplate* (recall Samuel Alexander) Herrick viewing those clothes, then we cease to *enjoy* Julia's movement, which would be a sorry shame.

As Lewis puts it: 'I do not owe the poet some aesthetic response: I owe him love, thanks, assistance, justice, charity—or it may be, a sound thrashing.' And there we have both Lewis's severity—a distinction that will remain distinctive—and a bedrock principle: treat the thing in its quiddity, its *thingness*. A poem is not a personal profile.

The second book is, as Lewis avers, adversarial. He is offended by the dismissive criticism directed at Shelley, William Morris, the alliterative metre of Anglo-Saxon poetry, and the new English syllabus (which he had a hand in formulating). In 'Variations in Shakespeare and Others' we read that Will 'darts at the subject and glances away; and then he is back again before your eyes can follow him'. Lewis makes comparisons to Milton, Yeats, and others, none of which redound to the Bard's credit. In the final essay, 'Christianity and Literature', Lewis admonishes that 'it is not hard to argue that all the greatest poems have been made by men who valued something else much more than poetry'. But the antepenultimate essay, 'Bluspels and Flalansferes: A Semantic Nightmare', is the one to read if you read no other. 'Imagination is the organ of meaning', Lewis teaches, and 'reason the organ of truth', and he shows us why.

The Allegory of Love

A landmark of literary history, this book (1936) won the prestigious Gollancz Prize and established Lewis as among the major literary medievalists in the world. He is now of the elect. Moreover, among its great achievements is its accessibility, not merely to other scholars but to any literate reader.

Lewis's argument is simple. The Middle Age brings a new kind of romance, that between a devoted lover (probably a knight) and his lady, who must not be his wife. He swears fealty and does heroic deeds on her behalf, but his love is not to be confused with married love, which comes later. Thus do we have courtly love. Then Lewis establishes allegory, a genre that uses physical entities to represent immaterial states, the device we've seen in *The Pilgrim's Regress* where, for example, the character of Wisdom makes an appearance. To consolidate the two (courtly love and allegory) he enthusiastically examines the fundamentally influential *Romance of the Rose*. The third step is to apply the first two to literary examples, especially Chaucer's *Troilus and Criseyde* and Spenser's *The Faerie Queene*. His telling distinction (he loves distinctions, remember) is that between allegory (representation by the less real, like the *character* of hate) and symbolism (or 'sacramentalism'), which points to the more real.

Lewis's dear friend and colleague Neville Coghill captures Lewis's true genius so evident in this book: '[his] power to make…generalizations that lead the reader into new territory'. In that light, consider the following as an example of Lewis's style. 'Thus *Troilus* is what Chaucer meant it to be—a great poem in praise of love. Here also, despite the comic and tragic elements, Chaucer shows himself, as in the *Book of the Duchesse*, the *Parlement*, and the *Canterbury Tales*, our supreme poet of happiness.' There is a generalization for the ages. The periodic structure of the second sentence (we must wait for the punchline) coming after the alliterative bounce of the first is hard to resist. But the paragraph goes on for another *twenty-seven lines*, almost the whole of the page. Here is how it ends: 'the wild Provencal vine has begun to bear such good fruit that it is now worth taming', a fitting metaphor.

'Learning in War-Time' and 'Transposition'

Very different in tone are his sermons. Though some are lost, seven have been published in various collections. 'Learning in War-Time', Lewis's first, was preached to a packed house at the Church of St Mary the Virgin on 22 October 1939. I've already mentioned it, but a bit more needs saying. England is at war, and everyone knows the misery to come. Nevertheless, that state of affairs matters *less* than meets the eye. 'He who surrenders himself without reservation to…temporal claims…is rendering to Caesar that which…belongs to God: himself.' Lewis emerges as the master of perspective.

'Transposition' (1944) treats a genuinely fundamental feature of Lewis's thinking. His discussion begins with 'a stumbling block', in fact, 'an embarrassing phenomenon', that of *glossolalia*, or speaking in tongues. He places the difficulty into a larger category that includes erotic imagery in the Bible. The problem is 'that of the obvious continuity between things…admittedly natural and things which…are spiritual; the reappearance in…our spiritual life of all the same old elements which make up our natural life'. He allows that sceptics have a good case: supernatural belief copies the natural world (as the queen claims in *The Silver Chair*). The senses compensate for this disparity by using the same sensations to express more than one emotion, even opposite emotions. Here exactly is *transposition*, the rendering into a poorer language a world too rich for direct translation; 'if you are making a piano version of a piece originally scored for an orchestra', Lewis

THE PROBLEM OF PAIN

C. S. LEWIS

Fellow of Magdalen College, Oxford

THE CHRISTIAN CHALLENGE SERIES

5. The cover of *The Problem of Pain*.

writes, then the same piano notes which represent flutes in one passage must also represent violins in another.

The relation of the higher to the lower is 'sacramental' and the lower can be drawn into the higher; the sensation of joy, for example, can itself become joy. That, he tells us, is how the Incarnation of Christ worked, not by 'the conversion of the Godhead into flesh, but by the taking of Manhood into God'. Those who are blind to this phenomenon are like a dog that stares at a pointing finger rather than understanding that it points at something else.

The Problem of Pain

Given a God both loving and omnipotent, why does He allow pain to afflict the undeserving? Lewis's answer is less a case than a discussion (see Figure 5). Original Sin has moved us from master of the house to a lodger, even to a prisoner, in the home intended for our ownership. In that light, as God's megaphone to a deaf world, pain warns us of our sinfulness. Still, we err in thinking of Him, not as the Father but as the spoiling Grandfather, confusing kindness with divine Love. And this: we are members of one organism, beholden to each other for better *and* worse. His final chapter, 'Heaven', anticipates the beckoning imagery of 'The Weight of Glory', with Lewis striking a recurring note: 'The thing you long for summons you away from the self.' The book was well received; that he settled the question remains in dispute.

Evacuated children arrive from London; Lewis tutors one mentally challenged child, another becomes a successful actress and lifelong friend to the brothers; Charles Williams moves to Oxford; Warnie is recalled to duty (he will be at Dunkirk, eventually discharged as a major); and Maureen Moore marries, later becoming Lady Dunbar of Hempriggs. There must never have been a dull moment.

Chapter 4
Fame

Two quotations set the stage for Lewis in the 1940s. To his
friend Sister Penelope of the Sisters of St Mary the Virgin,
he writes, 'any amount of religion can now be smuggled in
under the guise of fiction'; that is the basis of the Ransom
Trilogy (named after its hero, Elwin Ransom). The second,
from his Preface to *Mere Christianity*, is, 'I have thought
that the best, perhaps the only, service I could do for my
unbelieving neighbours was to explain and defend the
belief that has been common to nearly all Christians at
all times.'

One, two, many Lewises

Those beliefs give rise to his vocation as an apologist. After
The Problem of Pain come *The Screwtape Letters* (a diabolical
correspondence, no less, 1942) and his vastly popular BBC talks
(four series occurring in 1941, 1942 twice, and 1944, with an
average of 1.2 million listeners per broadcast), thereafter
published as three slim books, *Broadcast Talks* (1942), *Christian
Behavior* (1943), and *Beyond Personality* (1944, all to be
consolidated and edited by Lewis as *Mere Christianity*, 1952).
He tours Royal Air Force bases giving talks to airmen, and
though he thinks these unsuccessful he learns much about the
popular use of language.

Amid prodigious letter-writing (in the *Collected Letters* the 1940s require 699 pages, nearly double the number from the 1930s), he continues the tradition of walking tours with Warren and others from the 1930s, converses (notably with the Inklings) while drinking beer and smoking cigarettes and his pipe and hearing the exuberant anti-Catholic and anti-*Lord of the Rings* Hugo Dyson shout, 'not another f***ing elf!' Without the presence of Lewis and the Inklings we simply would not have Tolkien's *The Lord of the Rings*. He writes poems, of course, and publishes seventy-three scholarly, religious, and cultural essays—*and* teaches and lectures. In 1942 Stella Aldwinkle founds the Socratic Club, where Christians take on all comers in weekly debate. ('We are not impartial, but argument is.') Lewis, a frequent presenter, would be its president from 1942 to 1954 (Figure 6).

A Preface to 'Paradise Lost' (1942), *The Great Divorce* (a bus trip to Heaven, 1946), and *Miracles* (1947), major accomplishments, add to the list of books written and published in the 1940s, during which he is also researching and delivering the Clark Lectures, to become the massive *English Literature in the Sixteenth Century, Excluding Drama* (1954), and the Riddell Memorial Lectures (1943), which will become *The Abolition of Man* (1943). Near the end of the decade come *Arthurian Torso* (1948, a study of the poetry of his friend Charles Williams), and *Transposition and Other Addresses* (a collection of sermons, 1949). In 1947 he publishes *George MacDonald: An Anthology*, the thirteenth book of this period. It is an exhausting pace.

The Screwtape Letters

On 21 July 1940, a Sunday, Lewis was attending the Communion service at Holy Trinity Church, his parish in Headington Quarry, Oxford. Sometime during that service he was struck by the notion for a book of letters from a senior devil, Screwtape, to an apprentice tempter, his nephew Wormwood, in which he would examine the 'psychology of temptation from the *other* point of

C. S. Lewis

6. Jack (left) and brother Warnie on a walking tour.

view'. Lewis would deliver all thirty-one letters by Christmas to *The Guardian*, a religious weekly Anglican newspaper that published them serially from May through November of 1941, during the darkest days and nights of the London blitz. Uncle Screwtape was an immediate hit.

In these intercepted letters, we have secret information about us, we 'patients' in the language of Hell, who would be food for 'our father below'. A young man, in a big city during wartime and unbeknownst to him, is under spiritual attack by Wormwood, who is both invisible and inaudible to the young man. The tempter can influence the man's intellect and imagination but cannot work directly on his will; the man is always a free agent. But Wormwood is something of a bumbler, and Uncle Screwtape is increasingly undone, finally turning into a centipede.

Each letter provides insight into some psychological, moral, or theological reality. Love is not a storm of emotion (no. 18); evil is parasitic (no. 9): 'I know we have won many souls through pleasure. All the same it is His invention, not ours: all our research so far has not enabled us to produce one'; God is a 'hedonist' at heart (no. 22). Or this from no. 8: 'Do not let him suspect the law of undulation. Let him assume that the first ardours of his conversion might have been expected to last' so that he is in doubt when they do not. The patient should pay very much attention to his own feelings.

Finally, the patient becomes a Christian: 'He saw Him. This animal, this thing begotten in a bed, could look on Him....Once more the inexplicable meets us...If only we could find out what He is really up to?' As for Wormwood? The book ends with, 'Most truly do I sign myself, Your increasingly and ravenously affectionate uncle, Screwtape.'

When asked how he knew so much about temptation, Lewis answered, 'I just looked into my own mind and heart'.

A Preface to 'Paradise Lost' and The Abolition of Man

At the age of nine Lewis wrote that he had read *Paradise Lost*, 'with reflections there-on'. He would reread it over and again in his teens. On 1–3 December 1941, he delivered the Ballard Mathews Lectures at University College of North Wales, warning his host that he had much to say in this *Preface*, in which Lewis means to describe the prerequisite assumptions to understanding Milton's epic. He open his *Preface* with, 'the first qualification for judging any piece of workmanship... is to know what it is—what it is intended to do and how it is meant to be used'. From there Lewis proceeds to teach, not only Milton's poem, but a conception of epic poetry generally, literary criticism even more generally, and then no small amount of philosophy and theology.

After distinguishing types of epic, Lewis lambasts poets who write only for other poets: 'The republic of letters resolves itself into an aggregate of uncommunicating... monads; each... mitred himself Pope and King of Pointland.' Then comes his major distinction, that between Primary (Homer, *Beowulf*) and Secondary (Virgil) epic. He discusses the content and style of the first—supposed history told effectively with stock images—then proceeds to Virgil's *Aeneid*. There, according to Lewis, we see the poet virtually reinventing the epic, one elegantly phrased and avowedly based on legend. *Paradise Lost* is a secondary epic, but he also insists that 'a certain elementary rectitude of human response is "given" by nature herself, and may be taken for granted'. Later he insists, 'we need most urgently to recover the lost poetic art of enriching a response without making it eccentric, and of being normal without being vulgar'. He will refute a number of charges against Milton, such as the one claiming that the poet made Satan more heroic than he intended. Rather, claims Lewis, Satan goes from 'hero to general, from general to politician, from politician to secret service agent, and thence to a thing that peers in at bedroom or bathroom windows, and thence to a toad, and finally to a snake'.

At the heart of the book is Lewis's defence of hierarchy ('if you will not obey authority you will find yourself obeying brute force') and his plausible defence of the Fall, which Milton and St Augustine view similarly. But in the ninth of nineteen chapters comes his explication of the 'Unchanging Human Heart' and of its importance. Yes, he allows, we, like the ages in which we live, are, at bottom, the same, but that is the *very* bottom. Above that level differences matter, and we should apply that idea to Milton's theology. 'To enjoy our full humanity we ought...to contain within us potentially at all times...all the modes of feeling and thinking through which man has passed.' Or, to say it otherwise, we must get beyond our times and our self. At the end Lewis refutes the charge of unreality in Milton, discerning fundamental differences, not merely of values or sensibility but of a conception of consciousness (reason versus instinct) that separates him from us.

The *Preface* and *The Abolition of Man* stem from those same premises respecting selfhood and reason. In both, Lewis's debating skills are in full sail. Yet *Abolition* is one-third as long as the *Preface* and reads like a lawyer's opening, where the case is stated but not made. As seminal and influential as it is, it is too short.

The three sections of *Abolition* are 'Men Without Chests', 'The Way', and 'The Abolition of Man', all followed by an inventory of moral values shared by cultures diverse in time and place; it is the Natural Moral Law that includes, for example, the Law of Mercy from Hindu, Babylonian, and Norse cultures, and Duties to Parents, Elders, and Ancestors from the Ancient Jewish, Greek, and American Indian cultures.

In the first part Lewis explains that in previous ages the chest was considered the seat of proper sentiment; that is, sentiment that was *ordinate* (fitting) with the stimulus to which a person responded. But, he says, those sentiments need to be trained—and that training is now missing. The villain here is subjectivism. Rather than recognizing the objectivity of a value (whether aesthetic or moral) people have fallen back on their feelings. (Later Lewis will tell us that 'feelings come and go; mostly they go'.) In short, we have internalized features outside of ourselves: the waterfall is 'sublime' becomes we have 'sublime feelings', with the self originating and validating the sublimity—which Lewis thinks is nonsense, since the ordinate response to sublimity is humility. He concludes the section by saying, 'we make men without chests and expect of them virtue and enterprise.... We castrate and bid the geldings be fruitful.'

The second section is a statement, and defence, of our shared Natural Law (the Tao, or the Way). It is not of our invention but a set of values embedded in Reason itself. Lewis then identifies the Innovator as one who presumes to see through values as mere conventions: anything we are told we *ought* to do is, at best, non-rational, there being no pre-existing ground for the moral command. Instead, the Innovator relies upon instinct. There is no *objective* moral code outside ourselves, so we fall back on what is inside. The problem here, however, is that instincts compete with each other, and so finally there must be an appeal to some outside arbiter—an objective code through the back door. 'The rebellion of new ideologies against the Tao is a rebellion of the branches against the tree.'

And that is exactly what the worst of us (those Conditioners) would have. Here Lewis attacks not science but 'scientism', the belief that nature should be utterly controlled and that humans are nothing more than an outgrowth of physical nature. Thus can the conditioner do as he pleases to people, just as he might to a tree or a rock. 'Man's conquest of nature, if the dreams of some scientific planners are realized, means the rule of a few hundreds of men over billions upon billions of men.'

Think of the Communist's 'New Man', or the billions of aborted children (who after all aren't 'persons'), or the eugenics practised on, and mass murder of, Jews before and during the Holocaust, or African slaves who were bred. Eventually, all morality is 'seen through'. But, says Lewis, 'if you see through everything then everything is transparent. . . . To "see through" all things is the same as not to see.'

The Great Divorce

Lewis then revisits fiction, this one another dream-vision as a vehicle for religious rather than philosophical thinking. Originally published in twenty-three instalments in *The Guardian*, from 10 November 1944 to 13 April 1945, the story is of passengers on a bus trip to the fringe of Heaven and the choices they make when offered an opportunity to enter. As with *Regress* and *Screwtape*, *The Great Divorce*, though oblique in manner (neither straightforward essay nor sermon), is heavily didactic. And as with those others metaphors and symbols convey meaning, a depiction of what *is*, while dramatic argument displays *truth*, that is, instruction. The self is a prison, and Hell is self-made, secured by a door locked on the inside. Our insubstantial reality of atoms and molecules is much less solid than the one our immortal soul is destined for, if we can escape from the self-serving nest of appetites that we think of as 'me'.

The naïve narrator finally settles into a bus queue after strolling along the dingy, rain-drenched streets of a city at dusk. He hears someone refer to his own death in the past tense. Many impatient people leave the line in frustration; they have dismissed rumours of where the bus is headed. Finally the narrator ('Lewis') gets on and the bus takes flight. When he looks down he sees a city of great expanse very far below. It keeps growing because people, not able to stand each other, move farther and farther away. On the bus he hears grumpiness from most of those around him—though not from the driver, who is bathed in bright glory. When the careering bus finally lands the passengers get off and disperse. They will discover that, even at this fringe of Heaven, reality is so substantial that the grass will not bend under their feet. At a river they find that they will not sink but be thrown off balance by a flow that is like a moving sidewalk. Rain drills through them. They are ghosts.

Soon they see figures approaching. These are Solid People who, having advanced deeply into Heaven, nevertheless have made the long trek back to persuade passengers—loved ones—to stay. There follow some half-dozen conversations overheard by the narrator. In each case the passenger is unwilling to surrender an appetite. One woman wants her husband back so that she can continue to mould him: she always knows best. Another cannot admit that a heavenly resident who was a murderer is not in the city below and so refuses to stay out of spite, he (the passenger) being so much the better person. A third (a dwarf holding a chain with a huge, posturing actor at the other end) cannot lay down his haughty projection in favour of humility; in fact, he refuses to answer his Solid Person because that Person insists on addressing the real passenger, the dwarf not the theatrical, self-inflated 'Tragedian'. Another passenger is the Episcopal Ghost, who would dearly love to stay but cannot because he is about to deliver a paper on how great Jesus would have been had he only lived past the age of thirty-three.

A young man, however, does stay, when he asks an angel to kill the lizard on his back, an action that will hurt the young man terribly. At that, the reptile turns into a beautiful white stallion that the young man mounts and rides on into Heaven. At one point a great lady, honoured by all, appears. Can she be the Virgin Mary? No. But she is one who, while unknown on Earth, was of inestimable virtue. Here, with proper moral and spiritual judgement restored (and our perception reversed, typically Lewisian), her great goodness is recognized.

The narrator has many questions as he strolls to meet George MacDonald, who explains that our perspective is far too limited to understand the questions let alone the answers. For example, when the narrator talks of the vastness of the city, MacDonald points out that all of it could fit into the smallest crack of the solid ground they are standing on. Presently the narrator awakes, frightened that the sun has risen before he could make his fateful choice. 'I awoke in a cold room, hunched on the floor beside a black and empty grate, the clock striking three, and the [air-raid] siren howling overhead.' The book is one of Lewis's shortest.

Other than books

Among his memorable essays of this period are 'Membership', 'Meditation in a Toolshed', and 'The Poison of Subjectivism'; of greater impact are two of his finest sermons, 'Transposition' and the pivotal 'The Weight of Glory'. No venue is too small or too narrow for his attention, for example, the *Bristol Diocesan Gazette* or the Electrical and Musical Industries Christian Fellowship. Moreover, no idea was too challenging: if Jesus promised His return during His own generation, why didn't He? If we are promised that, if we ask we shall receive, why don't we? If we are told to love our neighbours as we love ourself, why is self-regard so dangerous?

The second half of the 1940s is fraught. On 15 May 1945, Lewis suffers the death of his dear friend Charles Williams. ('When the idea of death and the idea of Williams thus met in my mind, it was the idea of death that was changed.') As the decade draws to a close he suffers with a mentally deteriorating Mrs Moore and worries over an increasingly alcoholic Warnie (the 'mother' and brother having warmed to each other when she taught him to play the piano). In 1946 he meets the well-regarded poet Ruth Pitter, with whom he maintains a steady correspondence. Later, Joy Davidman will come to dislike her intensely. (But for his own ill health, widower Lewis might have proposed marriage to Pitter in the 1960s.)

His energy has proven a match for the profusion of his ideas and language, what Barfield called his 'presence of mind', yielding a preternatural appetite for work, vocational commitment, professional diligence, and a mental resourcefulness that are staggering in their fertility. In that light we are about to see masterpieces. We know that Lewis would delight in writing the sort of literature he enjoyed reading. Nevertheless, what this lover of myth and of science fiction would produce is astonishing both in kind and quality.

A cosmic mythology

Lewis was a devoted reader of stories in American science fiction magazines (particularly the *Magazine of Fantasy and Science Fiction*). His essay 'On Science Fiction' (originally a talk given to the Cambridge University English Club in 1955) is literary criticism at its richest, and his own few stories (e.g. 'Forms of Things Unknown') are representative of his thinking; other writers, for example Brian Aldiss and Kingsley Amis (a 1962 conversation among the three men was first printed as 'Unreal Estates' in 1964), esteemed Lewis's 'speculative fiction'. Lewis was especially struck by Olaf Stapledon's *Last and First Men*, which takes our species very far into the future, and by H. G. Wells's *The First Men in the Moon*.

But Lewis had bigger fish to fry than the mere defiance of space and time. 'There is, then, a particular kind of story which has a value in itself...independent of its embodiment in any literary work. These stories...always have a very simple narrative shape—a satisfactory and inevitable shape, like a good vase or a tulip.' That is how Lewis describes myth. He goes on to say that myths are somehow fantastic, always grave, and that 'we feel it to be numinous'. He also says that 'the same story may be a myth to one man and not to another'. In his essay 'On Stories' Lewis shows his hand:

> No merely physical strangeness or merely spatial distance will
> realize that idea of otherness which is what we are always trying to

grasp in a story about voyaging through Space.... To construct plausible and moving 'other worlds' we must draw on the only real 'other world' we know, that of the spirit.

Out of the Silent Planet

Elwin Ransom, a philologist, is walking an unusually quiet countryside. It is late, and when he is refused hospitality at a nearly empty inn (a bad sign) he knocks at a cottage, meets a mother worried over her missing son Harry, and agrees to seek him at the cottage of 'the Professor and the gentleman from London'. They will turn out to be Weston and Devine, who would send the boy off in a rocket to Malacandra (Mars) as a sacrificial offering to ravenous creatures. When Ransom attempts to intervene, the two overcome him and put him into the rocket instead, and off goes Ransom into the void of Outer Space.

We see here two aspects of Lewis's method. The first is his working out of a 'supposal', as he calls it. Suppose there is intelligent life in the solar system beyond Earth. What would they be like? What might they think of us? What would they think of Earth, which will turn out to be, for very sinister reasons, the 'silent planet'? The second is Lewis's use of reversal, in this case of his hero's and our expectations. Outer Space is not a void but alive with light and life; the red planet is populated by three different species living in peace; the creatures to whom he was sent as a sacrifice, certainly frightening at first glance, are innocent, and our planet (known as Thulcandra) is quarantined because of its own Fall.

Lewis takes his vision farther still. His hero spends much time on Malacandra, comes to know its three species—*sorns*, *hrossa*, and *pfifltriggi*: all *hnau*, or possessed of reason—and their language (Old Solar), has adventures as well as misadventures as he experiences landscapes, customs, and virtues, and learns that the planet has a presiding spirit, an *eldil*, the *Oyarsa*, in the service of the greatest eldil, Maleldil, the creator.

A hilariously embarrassing confrontation has Weston and Devine (who have finally shown up) offering trinkets to the natives, but the exchange allows Oyarsa to know Weston and Devine for the self-interested schemers they are. Ransom learns that the reason for our isolation is the rebellion of *our* eldil against Maleldil; the quarantine, which makes our planet 'silent', is to keep our fallen eldil *in*. Now, with the violation of that quarantine by Weston and Devine, there is no telling the evil that may spread.

After a perilous journey back to Earth (during which Devine shows real courage), Ransom is back home and in a village street. 'A lighted door was open. There were voices from within and they were speaking English. There was a familiar smell.... "A pint of bitter, please," said Ransom', a conclusion in very stark contrast to the opening. In the final chapter we learn that Ransom has told Lewis his story, suggesting that now that the quarantine has been broken, more bravery beyond the orbit of the Moon (the original Thulandran 'fence') will be necessary.

Perelandra

Though the style of *Perelandra* is typically Lewis's (albeit more strikingly descriptive than any other of his works), its structure is not. Here presumably true events are directly related by a participant in those events. If there is any 'key' it lies in James George Frazer's study in comparative religion, *The Golden Bough*, which had impressed Lewis; universal archetypes abound. Now the reader decides: myth? or not myth?

On the plant Perelandra—our Venus, a multi-coloured, prismatically clouded paradise of water, floating islands, and Fixed Land, unspoiled by evil—there dwelt a Green Lady and her King. Maleldil, Maker of All Things, gave them all they could want, but He forbade them ever to remain on the Fixed Land during the night. The Green Lady and the King returned Maleldil's love and obeyed Him. Then it happened that the Lady and the King became separated. At that time the Dark Power of Earth, enemy of Maleldil and all of His creatures (and no longer quarantined), came to the Lady as the 'Un-man' (the scientist Weston who has welcomed possession by our fallen eldil). He tried to persuade her to disobey Maleldil, and he might have succeeded had not Ransom, one of Maleldil's loyal servants from Earth, intervened. In spite of the danger to himself and at the cost of great suffering, Ransom fought the Dark Power and drove him into the Deep. And so it came to pass that the Green Lady and the King, because they had not disobeyed Maleldil, were raised to high glory as the Father and Mother of a new Beginning. This was told by the man called Ransom.

That Hideous Strength

Lewis seems always to have had some piece of writing in the works. This was true of *The Chronicles*, his autobiography, a narrative poem, and of *Abolition* (to which this book is the fictional correlative). The continuity of his labours, especially in light of the scraps of paper he wrote on, is hard to fathom. This book, too, had a false start. It is by far the longest of the three and the most complexly plotted, as thrillers will be. It is set on Earth, and in addition to its thrills (maximized by cross-cuts, close calls, and other devices, all well managed) is marked by sheer horror. Thus its subtitle: 'A Fairy-Tale for Adults'.

Jane Studdock is a doctoral student who cannot get on with her thesis. Her husband Mark is a Fellow of Sociology at Bracton College in Edgestow, a Midlands village. He badly wants to be among the 'progressive element' (an 'inner ring' about which Lewis will write). Jane, on the other hand, is troubled by a dream: a man's head has been twisted off and kept alive and people are digging up an ancient figure, 'a druidical kind of man'.

Mark meets Lord Feverstone (Devine, from *Out of the Silent Planet*), who enlists him to write press stories on behalf of the

College; these will be largely false. As it happens, Feverstone and other sinister (and quite haunting) figures are part of N.I.C.E., the National Institute of Coordinated Experiments—all very scientific. Meanwhile, Jane, troubled by her dreams, seeks out Mother Dimble, whose husband was Jane's tutor and is an authority on the Arthurian legend. She recommends to her that she visit St Anne's on the Hill to meet none other than Ransom, who has not aged but had been wounded by the bite of the Un-man. He is the Pendragon, the heir to King Arthur's authority.

From this point forward the action shifts between the College, where 'man has got to take charge of man . . . some men have to take charge of the rest', and Ransom's community of organic friendship (including Mr Bultitude, a bear), with him as the Head. But N.I.C.E. is keeping another head alive, that of a criminal who was decapitated, the very head of which Jane dreamt. That head will be the portal for malignant powers that descend, the fallen *eldila* (the plural of 'eldil') who will help establish this scientific order. The villains expect the help of Merlin, who lies in a nearby wood. (In a hilarious sequence, the N.I.C.E. mistakes a hobo for the great mage.)

Mark is sorely tested, especially in a room of grotesque abnormalities, Jane is estranged from him, and Merlin (who, though primitive, is righteous) will bring mayhem to the N.I.C.E., casting a spell that transforms language into babble. Meanwhile, owing to the breach of the quarantine around Earth at the orbit of the Moon, good *eldila*—in fact gloriously terrifying angels—descend on St Anne's on the Hill. Belbury, the centre of N.I.C.E. wrongdoing, is destroyed by an earthquake, Jane and Mark are reunited happily, and the *eldila* transport Ransom (his work as the Pendragon now done) back to Perelandra, where his wound will heal.

Finally we understand what is at stake. Earth may be one small part of a larger design, yet the reader sees with fresh eyes the

7. The cover of the first edition of Warren's diary, Jack on the left.

enormity of the Fall and the magnitude of the forces that range both against us and for us. Lewis's own power is formidable: horror is abysmal, satire biting, fertility images lush, action gripping, themes daunting, and the holy numinous. The book is a page-turner; that there are too many pages is evidenced by the fact that Lewis himself condensed it under the title *This Tortured Planet*. Some believe this to be Lewis's 'Williams novel', a 'spiritual thriller' of the sort Lewis (and T. S. Eliot) admired so greatly.

A wave breaks

Lewis's correspondence becomes overwhelming, sometimes arriving at the rate of several hundred letters per week. Only Warren's help makes answering all of them possible, but Lewis is never dismissive or curt and is always deeply grateful for the steady flow of food (for example, canned hams) that begins to arrive (Figure 7). Some correspondents, especially Americans, become regular pen pals. His pen-friendship with Sister Penelope deepens, and his Latin correspondence with Father Calabria begins on 6 September 1947; Lewis will depend on both friends, though differently. On 8 September 1947, he appears on the cover of *Time* magazine with a caricatured Uncle Screwtape balanced on his left shoulder. The caption reads: 'His heresy: Christianity'. He seems at the height of his powers, his ideas and energy abounding (see Box 2).

Box 2 Ten key ideas from Lewis's works

These are central to Lewis's thinking: many of his arguments are based upon them and they were central to his life. Omitted are orthodox Christian ideas (e.g. the Incarnation), as well as political ones (e.g. the danger of fetishizing equality: 'I'm as good as you').

Joy (*Sehnsucht*) is a longing conveyed by some image or memory or event that does not originate in any of those but comes through them. It is from a place beyond the senses and kindles a *hope* that there is Heaven, that Heaven is our home, and that we will return there. It is painful because nothing in this world can satisfy it, no matter how hard we may try to do so; it is *sweetly* painful because we can intuit its origin and our destiny.

Contemplation and Enjoyment (or At/Along), or knowing from the outside and from the inside, where a phenomenon (such as religious belief or being in love) may seem very different. We need both.

Chronological snobbery is the uncritical acceptance of our own intellectual climate, as though past beliefs or practices are useless simply because they came before us. A corollary is that our belief in Progress is misplaced: we must ask what it is we are 'progressing' towards.

Subjectivism is poisonous because it leads to an exaltation of the Self, a form of idolatry, especially when applied to morality, as when something is deemed good because it feels good.

Reason is objectively valid and, though one's logic may be flawed in any given case, is a sign of our non-material nature: atoms moving randomly in our brains is not thought. It is the 'organ of truth'.

Morality is objective, outside of any personal preference or perception and accessible to Reason. To be subjective respecting

(*continued*)

Box 2 Continued

this Natural Law (the Tao) is to submit to those who have the power, especially the technological power, to enforce their preferences, leading to 'the abolition of man'. It merits *obedience*.

Imagination, especially when realized as metaphor, symbol, and *myth*, is the 'organ of meaning', antecedent to truth. It helps extend language without distorting or destroying it ('verbicide')

Quiddity is the 'thingness' of a thing, be it a food, weather, or a person. We must pay attention to things as they are, name them appropriately, and respond *ordinately* to them.

Personhood is not at all the same as 'personality', the expression of which ought not to be one's goal; rather we should apply the *Law of Inattention*, allowing us to pay attention to all sorts of signs outside of the Self, especially to other people. What am I feeling? matters less than What *is* that? After all, 'feelings come and go, mostly they go'.

Ultimate Reality is not the plane of existence we occupy, which is but a 'shadowland', a sort of training camp for the realest thing. That *solid* place sends signs (e.g. Joy) and, because it is so much richer than our shadowland, must clothe those signs in words and objects that already have ordinary meaning to us (like erotic imagery symbolizing religious devotion). That is how *sacramentalism* works: a higher reality is *transposed* into a more limited key having 'notes' we recognize as ordinary.

Chapter 5
Darkness and light

Two weeks after his appearance on the cover of *Time*,
Lewis publishes 'Le Roi S'Amuse', a poem about a jubilant
Jove in the act of creation ending with 'Jove laughed to see | The
abyss empeopled, his bliss imparted, the throng that was
his and no longer he.' The writing of poetry remains his Little
End Room, while his heart and mind are soon on display
with two books.

George MacDonald: An Anthology

In his introduction to the anthology (1947) Lewis writes that he is
'discharging a debt of justice'. Of the 365 entries—the headings are
Lewis's own—only very few deal with feelings, including religious
feelings: 'a man does not live by his feelings any more than by
bread'. Others are about the concreteness of nature, self-control,
self-denial, pain, joy, and the like. One close to Lewis's heart is
'our Lord never thought to be original'. Entries on fear and dryness
are particularly telling: neither matters much. What do matter
are ideas such as these: 'Will is God's will, obedience is man's
will; the two make one', and 'continuity of existence . . . in itself
is worthless as hell'. The entries reveal the importance of the
collection: it is nothing less than a handbook of Lewis's
own thinking.

Miracles

As in *The Problem of Pain*, though in a tone more logically severe, Lewis uses a seven-step procedure: (1) frame the problem; (2) define terms; (3) address reservations, especially psychological ones; (4) address logical objections; (5) hypothesize an explanation for the phenomenon in question (the apparent defiance of physical laws, e.g. Jesus turning water into wine); (6) demonstrate the greater rationality of the new hypothesis over its competitors; and (7) make the alternative to disbelief imaginatively appealing.

Of the seventeen chapters, the first few are preparatory and refutative, and the final few take on specific miracles, including 'The Grand Miracle', the Incarnation. Those in the middle of the book assemble the premises that make the final few possible. For example, in 'Horrid Red Things' (chapter 10), he writes, 'thinking may be sound in certain respects where it is accompanied ... by false images [e.g. poison being deadly because of horrid red things inside of it]'.

Life off the printed page

Perhaps the most famous chapter Lewis ever wrote is from *Miracles*, chapter 3, 'The Self-Contradiction of the Naturalist'. In it Lewis makes an argument he would repeat often. The materialist (or 'naturalist') is one who believes that all reality is nothing more than matter (or physical nature); that is, energy and atomic and subatomic particles moving randomly. Lewis extends that argument to the brains of the people who make it. Are the mindless, purposeless atoms in their brains somehow gathering into a belief that is neither mindless nor purposeless?

At a meeting of the Socratic Club on 2 February 1948, Elizabeth Anscombe (who would become a world-famous Catholic philosopher) took Lewis to task on technical grounds, with particular emphasis on the difference between 'ground' and 'cause'. In a typically hyperbolic fashion, he used battlefield imagery to describe the encounter; Anscombe on the other hand did not see the exchange as particularly dramatic or damaging to Lewis's fundamental point. Still, Lewis clarified his terms in a revision of the chapter for a later edition.

The claim that the debate stopped Lewis from writing overtly apologetic work is preposterous; first, because he only wrote two such books (*The Problem of Pain* and *Miracles*), and, second, because other effusions were pressing at the gates of both his intellect and his imagination. He continues working on different projects simultaneously (and teaching and lecturing). All along his letters contain such wisdom as, 'what in Heaven's name is "distressing" about an old man saying to an old woman that they haven't much more to do here? ... I was referring to an obvious fact'.

Warren's scholarship on the Sun King deepened, and even as he worked on the Lewis Family Papers he wrote *The Splendid Century*, eventually published to considerable acclaim. One reader, a woman who had a deep interest in 17th-century France and had read the book in the late 1960s, wrote to Warren to thank him for it, adding, 'by the way, I believe you write better than your brother'. Walter Hooper would report that, upon reading the letter to Warren, he responded, 'there, Walter, you see that? Now that makes *two* of us!'

Lewis's home life, though, becomes increasingly unbearable, owing to the aged Mrs Moore's mental deterioration and the conflicts it causes. Ever more frequently Warren would take refuge, first in drink then with the nuns of Drogheda in Ireland to recover.

In 1951 Lewis turned down the offer of a knighthood from Churchill's second government: he did not want to be thought

8. A page from the manuscript of *The Screwtape Letters*.

politically compromised—or, he said, to be known as Sir Clive. (My own thinking is that the rejection had to do with Churchill's support of empire, which Lewis did not share.) His Latin correspondence with Father Calabria grows. Because neither Father Calabria nor Lewis could write fluently in the other's language, they wrote in Latin, and these *Latin Letters of C. S. Lewis* (1999), extending from 1947 to 1954, become among the most intimate Lewis ever wrote.

Soon Lewis faces a genuine spiritual crisis, with physical and emotional fatigue surely having played its part. On 14 January 1949, Lewis writes that his household is riven by women's disputes; worse, that he might never write another word, such is his 'accidia' (dryness and laziness); further, he is willing to pay that price because of the second sin (the first being the accidia) of pride arising from praise of his works. In 'The Apologist's Evening Prayer', written at this stage but unpublished in his lifetime, he begs God to 'take away my trumpery lest I die'. He seems to teeter on the brink of despair. By the end of the year, the manuscript of *The Lion, the Witch and the Wardrobe* (and other Narnia tales) is finished; as with many other books, it had been in the works for a long time.

In April of 1950 Mrs Moore (about whom, remember, he could not write in his autobiography) goes permanently to a nursing home, where Lewis visits every day. She dies on 12 January 1951. Within months something of great moment occurs. Years earlier he had written 'On Forgiveness' (not published during his lifetime), where he wrote that to refuse Christ's forgiveness is a sin—which is apparently exactly what he did. For it was not until a few months *after* Mrs Moore's death, in April 1951, that he believes his sins forgiven, saying as much to Father Calabria in a letter that December.

The character of his writing changes: its militancy muted, its imaginative allure more pronounced, its urgency contained. He is relaxed and largely untaxed, his conscience at rest. The Socratic Club, the Inklings, the friendships, the robust routines of dinner parties in his rooms, late-night conversations, enjoyment of pets, good health, tutoring and lecturing, and of course writing and reading—all proceed unencumbered.

On 10 January 1950, Lewis receives a latter from one Joy Davidman Gresham, a Jewish New Yorker and former Communist from the Bronx who, owing in large part to the

books of C. S. Lewis, had converted to Christianity along
with her husband William.

Mere Christianity

If Lewis is known for a work other than *The Chronicles* it is likely
this one (with *Screwtape* third). In a letter of 7 February 1941, he
was invited to broadcast on Christianity by J. W. Welch, director
of the BBC's Religious Broadcasting Department. Based upon
those talks, *Mere Christianity* has not only been purchased,
translated, and relied upon more than any of his works but has
catalysed many conversions. Its four 'books' are 'Right and Wrong
as a Clue to the Meaning of the Universe', 'What Christians
Believe', 'Christian Behaviour', and 'Beyond Personality: Or, First
Steps in the Doctrine of the Trinity'. Three features require
mentioning prior to a discussion of the book.

First, its Christianity is *mere*, an adjective borrowed from
Richard Baxter's *Church-History of the Government of Bishops*
(1689), in which he writes, 'I will tell you, I am a CHRISTIAN,
a MEER CHRISTIAN.... I am of that Party which is so against
Parties...that which by Christ and the Apostles has left to the
Catholic Church, or the Body of Jesus Christ on Earth.' A perfect
fit for Lewis, who in his essay 'Christian Apologetics' had declared
his purpose: 'We are to defend Christianity itself—the faith
preached by the Apostles, attested by the Martyrs, embodied by
the Creeds, expounded by the Fathers.'

The second feature is that the book is structured very like a
catechism. Each of its books has five, five, twelve, and eleven
chapters respectively, with titles such as 'We Have Cause to
be Uneasy', 'Rival Conceptions of God', 'Sexual Morality', and
'Nice People or New Men'.

The third feature is that it does not *feel* like a catechism. For
example, it begins, 'Everyone has heard people quarrelling'. In that

opening lies the essential appeal of this book. Its words are never technical, its sentences are short, the tone familiar. Lewis not only refers to himself (as a former atheist, for example) but directly addresses the reader. Most appealing are his analogies: the Trinity is like a lighted lamp with its glaring bulb, the rays from that bulb, and the pool of light made by those rays on a surface. He never admonishes. In fact, he advises that those who 'do not believe in permanent marriage' will do better by living together unmarried, for 'unchastity is not improved by adding perjury'. Nor should the state impose religious views on its citizens; after all, he would not care for Muslims telling him not to drink alcohol. Moreover, a thoroughly Christian society would be what is called Leftist, that is, Socialist.

And never is there anything (anywhere in Lewis) approaching this, from the Puritan American Colonial Jonathan Edwards: 'The bow of God's wrath is bent, and the arrow made ready on the string, and justice bends the arrow at your heart, and strains the bow, and it is nothing but the mere pleasure of God, and that of an angry God...that keeps the arrow one moment from being made drunk with your blood.'

In his final chapter, 'The New Men', he compares the transformed person to a winged horse (having told us that the new step in evolution has already occurred, but from the top down instead of from the bottom up). Then he turns to the Self, 'At the beginning I said there were Personalities in God. I will go further now. There are no real personalities anywhere else.' That prepares the reader for his conclusion: 'Look for yourself, and you will find in the long run only hatred, loneliness, despair, rage, ruin, and decay. But look for Christ and you will find Him, and with Him everything else thrown in.'

A rush of events

On 3 March 1952 Lewis's spiritual director, Father Walter Adams, dies. *Mere Christianity* is published on 7 July 1952. (Two of the

Narnia books had already been published.) On 24 September 1952, the Lewis brothers meet Joy Gresham for lunch at the Eastgate Hotel; in December she and her two sons spend two weeks at the Kilns during the Christmas season. She was academically precocious, an award-winning poet, and a novelist. She returns to America in January of 1953 but is back in England with her two sons that November and rents a house in London. In mid-December she and her sons visit the Kilns.

Meanwhile Lewis is offered and, after much persuasion by Tolkien (who partly engineered the offer), accepts the position of Professor of Medieval and Renaissance Literature at Magdalene College (same saint, different spelling, this one 'repentant', according to Lewis), Cambridge University—an enormous decision. He had turned down the offer on the grounds of inconvenience; then, unbeknownst to Lewis, Dame Helen Gardner accepted. When Lewis changed his mind something unspeakably rare in the jealous halls of academe happened: Dame Helen withdrew.

Lewis would never learn of that. He had been passed up for other professorships, most famously that of Professor of Poetry, won by C. Day-Lewis, a former member of the Communist Party who never renounced communism and, more to the point, whose views on literature and criticism were close to those of C. S. Lewis. Many believe that Lewis was being punished, both for the semi-prank of having had Adam Fox elected years earlier and for his popularity outside the university as a Christian writer. Lewis himself joked that the loss was owing to a confusion of names.

Officially liberated from tutoring on 4 June 1954, Lewis will continue to live in Oxford, travelling back and forth by train (the 'Cantab Crawler'). In September his massive literary history, *English Literature in the Sixteenth Century, Excluding Drama*, is published. Of course, the Inklings continue to meet. On 29 November he delivers *De Descriptione Temporum*, his inaugural address. On 3 December, he conducts his last tutorial at Oxford, and in 1955 he is elected a member of the British Academy and *Surprised by Joy* is published. On 16 March 1956, *The Last Battle*, the seventh and final volume of *The Chronicles*, is published.

English Literature in the Sixteenth Century and *De Descriptione Temporum*

When it came to conveying 'the faith preached by the Apostles' he was not 'his own man', though in *private* practice he was (for example, confessing his sins aloud to a priest, abstaining from eating meat on Fridays, and praying for the dead). In his professional life, however, the opposite was the case: there his professional opinion *is* his business, and there he was very much his own man.

Lewis had been lecturing on the content of his great history for decades; the result is by far the longest book in the Oxford History of English Literature series. After its 558 pages of text come thirty-five pages of concurrent chronological tables, ninety pages of categorized bibliography, and eight double-column pages of index. The amount of reading Lewis did is staggering, that he marshals that reading into a virtual narrative (with the apt anecdote, quotation, or citation ready at hand), and that he sat and wrote, not only the book but more than 130 pages of highly detailed end matter, is unfathomable.

Ironically (I think) the table of contents is deceptively simple. Following 'Introduction: New Learning and New Ignorance' are three books: Late Medieval, 'Drab', and 'Golden', the first divided into two subsections, the second and third books into three each (the inverted commas being Lewis's own). The book proper ends with 'Epilogue: New Tendencies'. Already in the table we see the first sign of Lewis's revisionism, as he describes (he insists he is not judging) a half-century of English literature as *drab*. In Book III, he offers one section each on prose and verse, but the first section is devoted to 'Sidney and Spenser'—not Shakespeare.

Catholics are often 'Papists', along the way we get an endorsement of Purgatory (but not the horrifying version of Thomas More, whom Lewis clearly dislikes), and we learn that 'the exaltation of virginity is a Roman, that of marriage, a Protestant, trait', which must call to mind Lewis's gift for great generalizations. And everywhere is his characteristically direct style: the man who has passed through conversion feels like 'an accepted lover, he feels he has done nothing, and never could have done anything, to deserve such astonishing happiness'.

His discussion of Richard Hooker (especially his *Of the Lawes of Ecclesiastical Politie*) is revelatory. Hooker's eloquence 'is perfectly subdued to the task; [its] high mettle shows through [its] obedience.... And always, drawn in by the very genius of his philosophy, there is a sense of "the beautiful variety of all things".' Everywhere there is literary, historical, and theological context efficiently proffered. Though often broad, Lewis's judgements are never merely peremptory and are always engaging. Others have disagreed since, but none has matched Lewis's sweep, genius for comparison, or presence of mind when buttressing an argument.

Just as his magisterial history demonstrates Lewis's gifts of generalization and fluency, so does his inaugural lecture, with the added feature of a commanding perspective; he is contemplating *and* enjoying at the same time. Its historical sweep, exposure of the dangers of linguistic distortions and changes in modes of governance, his analytical precision, and his radical conclusion (in effect, not only did the Renaissance not happen, but no historical divide in the past has been as rupturing as that which divides us from the beginning of the 19th century, with the advent of the machine)—all take a mere fourteen pages marked by arresting analogies, challenging judgements, and self-deprecating wit.

Consider this, in response to the charge that, in a post-Christian age, we are relapsing into Paganism: 'It would be pleasant to see some future Prime minister trying to kill a large and lively milk-white bull in Westminster Hall' as a pagan ruler would have done. And this, in describing a post-Christian man, 'you might as well think that a married woman recovers her virginity by divorce'. And finally, when describing himself as an Old Western man, a 'dinosaur': 'If a live dinosaur dragged its slow length into the laboratory, would we not all look back as we fled?' After all, 'I may yet be useful as a specimen'. It is a *tour de force.*

Of other worlds

In August of 1954 Joy and Bill Gresham divorce. Eight months later Lewis and Joy wed in the registry office, presumably to prevent her deportation. Very few of Lewis's friends (whom he sees less of) like the brash, often vulgar woman. One year later Joy is dying of cancer. In great pain and with perhaps days to live, she and Lewis are married at her hospital sickbed by Father Peter Bide who, with a healing touch, lays hands upon Joy to restore her decayed pelvis and to ask that Lewis take her pain. In fact, he does, as Joy's hip is restored and she recovers. The doctors had no explanation. A brand new life for the Lewis brothers (Warren would remain resident with the family) is underway. Even as the Kilns is renovated, Lewis is heard to say, 'I never thought to have at sixty what passed me by in my twenties'.

The Chronicles of Narnia

'It All Began With a Picture', Lewis titled an essay: a faun carrying an umbrella and gifts through a snowy wood. There was no Aslan. Then the lion came 'bounding into it' and pulled the first story (*The Lion, the Witch and the Wardrobe*) together and the other six behind him. He had begun writing a fragment in 1939; between the summer of 1948 and March 1950, he completed five books. *The Magician's Nephew* gave him some pause, so he set it aside to write *The Last Battle*. Tolkien disliked them intensely, but Roger Lancelyn Green proved the ideal reader, critic, and catalyst and influenced some revisions. By February 1953 all seven books were done.

Of course, Lewis was again writing what he liked to read, but he also had some steady beliefs about fairy tales, which he stated in 'Sometimes Fairy Stories Say Best What's to Be Said' and in 'On Three Ways of Writing for Children'. He refutes some objections to the genre, points out that originally they were not intended for children, and insists that 'anything no longer worth reading as an adult was not worth reading in the first place'.

Lewis's master, George MacDonald, wrote about the fairy tale that it 'cannot help have meaning....The best thing you can do for your fellow...is to wake things up that are in him.' G. K. Chesterton had already counselled that 'fairy-tales are as normal as milk or bread...its spirit is the spirit of folk-lore...the German for common sense....The fairy tale is full of mental health.' And a third thoughtful source for Lewis, Kenneth Grahame (*The Wind in the Willows*), adds, 'a dragon for instance is a more enduring animal than a pterodactyl; yet every honest person believes in dragons—down in the back kitchen of his consciousness'.

Narnia—with its creatures from fairy stories, legend, and folklore; its perils, wonders, and pitch-perfect cosiness—is another world, another space-time, strange yet familiar, and beckoning in its holiness, for there is Aslan, the great creator-lion. And it is accessible, as we learn very near the beginning of *The Lion, the Witch and the Wardrobe* (which was published first) when Lucy Pevensie passes through the back of the wardrobe and meets Tumnus the Faun, learning from him that she is in Narnia where, because of the rule of the White Witch, it is always winter but never Christmas.

There she and her older siblings (Peter, Susan, and Edmund, who finally believe her tale of another world) will meet Aslan. In spite of Edmund's treachery (because of which Aslan must sacrifice himself on the stone table), and with the help of many brave Narnian creatures (talking beasts of all sorts), they defeat the witch. Winter ends. The Pevensies become royalty in this recognizably medieval world, with Peter as the High King, for they are the Sons of Adam and Daughters of Eve whose arrival has been prophesied for a very long time.

The second book is *Prince Caspian*, which seems an ordinary tale of a royal uncle trying to take the throne from its rightful occupant, the prince of the title. But it is not ordinary. First, we learn that Narnian time is even more unlike ours than seemed to be the case in the first book; centuries have passed in Narnia. Second, Lewis portrays a land that has had its history taken from it: the Old Narnia of the first book is in hiding. Third, Lewis affirms the power of myth and legend. Doctor Cornelius, a combination of dwarf and human and Caspian's tutor, has told the boy those old stories (despite uncle Miraz's prohibition), causing Caspian to long for the real Narnia. He rebels against Miraz and blows the horn of an ancient Queen, none other than Susan. With that, the children are called from our world. Fourth, we meet Reepicheep, the 'gay and martial mouse', who will figure in other adventures. When Peter is about to do single combat with Miraz, the uncle's own men kill him. Narnia is restored.

The third book, *The Voyage of the 'Dawn Treader'*, is the most complex in plot and theme and, along with *The Magician's Nephew*, most touched by holiness. In it we meet Eustace Clarence Scrubb, a nasty Pevensie cousin who is drawn with them into Narnia aboard the *Dawn Treader*, captained by Caspian, now Caspian X. They must search the Eastern Seas beyond the Lone Islands to find the seven Narnian lords whom Miraz had sent away. Among other wonders, they find a dangerous island where dreams—not least one's nightmares—come true, an island of monopods where Lucy finds (to her dismay) the Magician's Book, and an island where Eustace turns into a selfish dragon; and they meet a star, Ramandu, who teaches them that burning gas is what a star is made of, not what it is. It is Reepicheep who, finally, will journey alone to Aslan's country, his heart's desire. Learning from Aslan that she will never return to Narnia, Lucy tells the lion, 'It isn't Narnia, you know.... It's you. And how can we live, never meeting you?' But Aslan reassures her, and the reader realizes that worlds may indeed be linked. Lewis's evocation of Hope is at its most palpable.

The *Silver Chair* may be the most grimly exciting, as well as the most deeply philosophical, of the series. Again a prince, one Rilian, has been dispossessed, in fact has disappeared; again the villain is a witch (the same witch?), though she walks the Earth beautifully. (Digory, in fact Professor Kirk from the first book, would say he'd never seen a woman more beautiful than the White Witch.) Eustace and Jill Pole are blown into Narnia by Aslan after being told to remember four signs, which they either forget or fail to recognize. They must find Rilian.

On their trek north they meet the marsh-wiggle Puddleglum, whose pessimism is exceeded only by his wisdom, and that by his unspoken bravery. After overcoming many dangers, not least the Giants who would cook and eat them, they make it to Underland, where they find the prince bound to a silver chair. Only then does he know who he is and that the witch holds him prisoner, this knowledge called lunacy by the witch. When the children release him the witch appears and, with the help of a magic spell, begins to sing that there is no sun, there is no Narnia, and that here is no Aslan: all, she says, are mere copies of titbits from the only real world, hers. This is too much for Puddleglum who at the cost of great pain breaks the spell and gives a magnificent speech ending, 'I will live like a Narnian even if there is no Narnia'. Rilian kills the witch, now a serpent, and escapes with Puddleglum and the children, but by going further down, where they see another world altogether. (Lewis again playing with perspective.) Rilian learns that it was the witch who killed his mother. They return too late to see Caspian X before he dies, but Eustace and Jill do witness his resurrection by the blood of Aslan in the mountains overlooking Narnia.

The next book is *The Horse and His Boy*, a 'between-the-acts' tale occurring during the first reign of the Pevensies, directly after the action of the first book. Shasta, a Calormen slave, runs away, assisted by a talking Narnian horse, Bree. When King Edmund and Queen Susan visit Tashbaan, the capital of Calormen, there is a case of mistaken identity following Susan's refusal to marry Prince Rabadash (who eventually turns into a donkey). One Aravis, who has overheard plans of an invasion of Narnia and Archenland (it lies between Narnia and Calormen), runs away with Shasta and Bree to warn King Lune of Archenland. They are urged on by a lion who in the night seems like three lions to Shasta (Lewis's representation of the Holy Trinity). Narnians defeat the Calormens, and Shasta, who really is a prince, ascends to the throne.

Finally there are books six and seven that, in my opinion, belong together. *The Magician's Nephew* tells of the beginning of Narnia, *The Last Battle* of its end. Digory Kirk is the boy whom the Pevensie children will meet as an old man in *Wardrobe*. He and his neighbour Polly Plummer use magic rings made by Digory's uncle Andrew, who fancies himself a magician, to get to Charn, a world about to die. There Digory, too curious for his own good, awakens the witch Jadis (later the White Witch). She eventually follows the children, first back to London then to a place that is not yet a place—not until Aslan sings Narnia and Narnians into existence. Frank, a cabby who shared in the London adventure, says upon witnessing the creation, 'Glory be! I'd ha' been a better man all my life if I'd known there were things like this.' He and his wife become the first King and Queen of the new world, his horse Strawberry growing wings and becoming Fledge.

Adventures follow, the most important being Digory's entrance into a secret garden where there is an apple that could cure his dying mother. Jadis tempts him, but he resists, for to take the apple would be to disobey Aslan. But the lion gives him a slice to take back, and, when he gives it to his mother, she revives. The core of the apple is buried and grows into a tree. When a storm blows it down, it is made into the wardrobe.

One might expect that, after such wonders, *The Last Battle* would be troubling. Shift the ape, dressed in an old lion skin, parades as Aslan and deceives the population. Jewel the unicorn, Farsight the eagle, Roonwit the centaur, and King Tirian are despondent, as is poor Puzzle the deluded donkey. There is a battle in which old friends die, but finally, in a stable, all the kings and queens of Narnia we have known (but not Susan, who, as a young adult, has denied the existence of Narnia) are among those who believe in Aslan. They and others learn that Narnia was merely a copy—a Shadowland—and they enter a New Narnia. Lucy says the New Narnia has more colours and the mountains seem farther away, and Digory answers, 'more like the real thing'. Aslan leads them to the Garden of Paradise.

At the end a reader realizes that Narnia is not a different place but a different *kind* of place: its colours, contours, dryads, naiads, and other creatures; its marvels, perils, and perceptions, all road signs pointing us elsewhere. Those who do not see Lewis's veiled intent, and even those who come to resent it when they do, still would not escape its allure, though here I note the funniest and most outrageous criticism of the series. On a bookselling site a man who had eagerly looked forward to reading *The Chronicles* to his children did not, because he realized it was all a plot: Lewis was in collusion with the Cadbury company to sell Turkish Delight.

Chapter 6
A new day

In *The Chronicles*, Lewis comes as close to mysticism as he has in any other book, for Aslan, the holy of holies (as Lucy discerns), is the numinous made present. The same awe is stirred at the end of *Perelandra* by the Canticle of the Great Dance, or in some poems. 'And thus you neither need reply | Nor can; thus while we seem | Two talking', he concludes the poem 'Prayer', 'thou art one forever, and I | No dreamer, but thy dream.' That voice evoking joy will be ever with him (though not so much in his post-World War II letters, which deal with the quotidian, clarify literary matters, and dispense theological counsel: 'Do you know St. Francois de Sales' advice...meekness to God, to one's neighbour, and...to oneself?' he writes in 1958 to a Mr Pitman).

Though his apologetic writing becomes less polemical, a public not-avowedly Christian Lewis remains militant. His more than forty reviews, though never *ad hominem*, are often provocative, as when he calls Aristotle's *Poetics* a damaging book, or 'tragedy' a 'phantom' concept (in his 1962 review of George Steiner's *The Death of Tragedy*)—with no buttressing argument whatever (as there was when he dismissed the Renaissance). He has undergone many changes: near despair, forgiveness, marriage (surprising, desperate, joyful, and vexing to some friends), a monumental professional move, and a steady, but very new, rhythm, less urgent. We have been meeting a complex man, and he does not get simpler.

In Joy Davidman Lewis, Warren finds a drinking buddy. He would require trips to Ireland to dry out, once nearly converting to Catholicism. (A semi-panicked Lewis intervened and, according to Warren, got the worst of it in a debate with a Catholic priest there: his muted, vestigial bigotry admitted by Lewis would remain, and, oddly, it's one his critics never claim for him.) At Cambridge he makes new friends and enjoys himself. And he will revisit a piece of writing, a poetic fragment from 1923 called 'Cupid and Psyche', a myth that had deeply engaged him in his pre-Christian days. The result is his masterpiece (or so he, and others, believe), his one real novel (as opposed to allegory, fairy tale, or 'romance').

Till We Have Faces

Here I may only state a claim, not prove it. A simply written book with a complex structure, deliberately ambiguous imagery, a daunting theme, and a first-person narrator more interested in hiding than in revealing herself, this work is in fact a compendium of familiar Lewisian ideas but also a radical departure from anything he had written: substantively familiar, formally strange. Even many devoted Lewis readers disfavour it. And yet, once a reader puts away any prior Lewis and allows the novel to stand on it own, its high ranking as a major modern work is apparent, bearing comparison, not to other Lewis fictions but to those of Henry James, Woolf, Nabokov, and Faulkner.

In an ancient and primitive border kingdom having little intercourse with Greek learning and customs, Orual is the eldest daughter of King Trom of Glome, a man's man and a psychopath. Orual's younger sister, Redival, is vain and apparently disobedient. When their mother dies, the king takes a strange young bride who, after giving birth to a third (half-)sister, dies. That youngest sister is Psyche, beautiful and blessed. To the neglect of Redival, Orual will care for her obsessively. Trom buys a Greek slave, Lysias, called the Fox, who becomes the tutor and confidante of the sisters, with Redival always shunted aside.

When crops die and the population starves, Trom agrees to sacrifice Psyche (who has nursed the Fox back to health and is therefore thought to be divine) by delivering her to the Shadowbrute high on the mountain. The kingdom recovers, Trom dies, and Orual becomes Queen and, convinced (largely by Trom) that she is unendurably ugly, takes to wearing a veil. Her very capable general, diplomat, and warrior, Bardia, will teach her to use the sword, allowing that her shape and voice might make her marriageable.

She decides to recover the body of Psyche. Ascending the mountain with Bardia (who feeling the awfulness of the place hangs back) she comes to a promontory high above the kingdom. That new perspective allows her to see the world as beautiful. Her epiphany can be described only as Joy itself, but she denies it. (Psyche had once told her that when there she had felt that sweet longing.) She meets Psyche, who has not been devoured by a brute but has in fact married a god and lives in a palace, invisible to Orual.

The god has forbade Psyche to look upon him, and Orual, disbelieving her sister but jealous that someone else may have taken *her* Psyche, threatens to hurt herself, demanding that Psyche shine a light upon her husband. In an instant the god and the palace are visible to Orual—who again denies the reality of what she sees. Psyche, rejected, returns to Glome, where she will die. Orual spends decades as a very successful queen, making improvements to the kingdom and having conquests.

But she is miserable. She believes that her great misfortune is owing to the disfavour of the gods, who never show their faces. When Bardia dies, the widow stands up to Orual, recklessly cursing her. Instead of executing her (she has done as much in the past), Orual reveals her face; the widow sees that Orual, too, loved Bardia. People can get things wrong.

She sets to writing the complaint—'I am old now and have not much to fear from the anger of the gods' is her opening sentence—that becomes the first version of the story we have been reading. But when she decides to tour her kingdom she comes upon a priest who recounts the story of Psyche (the second version), in Orual's eyes getting it all wrong: there could *not* have been a god-husband and a palace. Moreover, she learns that Redival is not the character whom everyone took her to be but a lonely young girl neglected by her older sister: she succumbed willingly to a suitor who need not have been castrated. Orual again learns some truths that contradict her entire self-narrative.

C. S. Lewis

It gets worse. Orual's story is told a third time, the final version, this the real story, in a series of mystical visions. She sees herself as undertaking certain tasks that require her to substitute for Psyche. These tasks have symbolic content, of course, and Orual sees that the Fox, who has wept at the recitation of religious poetry but always rejected religious belief, was wrong. The meaning to which all our distorted tales point lies elsewhere, in another world we are meant to occupy and to which God has been calling us, in spite of our self-absorption. Finally, Orual hears a great voice tell her, 'you also are Psyche'. Instead of judging she is being judged; she cannot meet God face-to-face until she has her own.

Again Lewis will hasten a soul's progress by ending all talk. Orual dies in mid-sentence. 'You are yourself the answer. Before your face questions die away', she writes. 'What other answer

84

could suffice? Only words, words; to be led out to battle against other words. Long did I hate you, long did I fear you. I might—'.

Lewis would write a good deal about the book to various correspondents, trying to explain its complex quadruple helix of character, structure, themes, and symbols (amid the simplicity of voice). In yet another crypto-autobiographical work we have read a version of 'Lord of the narrow gate and needle's eye | take from me all my trumpery lest I die.' Reviews are favourable.

The public intellectual

Lewis's first published essay was 'The Expedition to Holly Bush Hill' in the *Cherbourg School Magazine* in 1912. The last one he prepared for publication is 'We Have No "Right to Happiness"' in late December of 1963 for the *Saturday Evening Post*. From 1932 to 1938 he published nine scholarly articles; then his focus shifted. 'Christianity and Culture' arrives in 1940, in *Theology*, very soon followed by 'The Dangers of National Repentance' and 'Two Ways with the Self' (*The Guardian*, also 1940). Several essays appear that will be incorporated into books (e.g. 'Horrid Red Things' into *Miracles*, and 'The Poison of Subjectivism' into *The Abolition of Man*). He has essays on 'Dogma and Science' (later, 'Dogma and the Universe') and on 'Equality'.

The venues vary enormously. In 1945 he publishes 'Meditation in a Toolshed' (*Coventry Evening Telegraph*) and 'Membership' (*Sobernost*). Moving into the late 1940s we get essays on Spenser, Joseph Addison (the early 18th-century essayist), and Kipling, but also others with titles like 'The Sermon and the Lunch', 'Notes on the Way' (one of which would become 'Priestesses in the Church'), 'On Living in an Atomic Age', and 'The Humanitarian Theory of Punishment'. With no respite the 1950s bring essays on Jane Austen, George Orwell, Dante, Walter Scott, and historicism; and others with such titles as 'Xmas and Christmas: A Lost Chapter from Herodotus', 'Prudery and Philology' (in *The Spectator*),

'Lilies that Fester', 'On Obstinacy in Belief' (*Sewanee Review*),
'Will We Lose God in Outer Space?' (later 'Religion and
Rocketry'), 'Willing Slaves of the Welfare State', and 'The Efficacy
of Prayer' (*Atlantic Monthly*).

It is useful to remember that life went on (professional, personal,
social) and that whole books were written at the same time, and
that this list is a mere sampling—as are the essays I discuss in the
next section. I just as well could have chosen 'Bulverism', 'Lilies
that Fester', or 'Is Theology Poetry?' in which Lewis tells us that
belief in Christianity is like going from a dream to waking; he
closes that with, 'I believe in Christianity as I believe that the
Sun has risen, not only because I see it, but because by it I see
everything else.' (In 'The Man Born Blind', a short story not
published during his lifetime, Lewis depicts a man whose sight is
restored and who, having heard about light, longs to see it, not
realizing that we see *by way of* light. He dies when he dives into
a pool of light refracted by a mist in a chasm.)

'Meditation in a Toolshed', 'Membership', and 'The Seeing Eye'

In 'Meditation in a Toolshed' Lewis provides a lesson in learning.
Once in a shed with a badly fitted door a sunbeam shone through
the crack. From a dark corner, Lewis could see the shape and
size of the beam and even dust particles floating within. But,
when he stepped into the beam, looking *along* instead of *at* it, the
world changed. Then not only did the dust disappear but the
beam itself, indeed the entire shed; there was nothing but light.
He could see the tree beyond the crack in the door and even the
sun beyond, the source of the beam. To know a truth one ought
to achieve both stances.

'Membership' (1945) considers the title conceptually and in its
application to Christians. Collective life is lower, argues Lewis,
than personal and private life. But radical individualism is far

worse than is membership in the Body of Christ. With that persons are like organs of one body—*not* interchangeable. Having argued that the place which the humblest Christian occupies is 'eternal and even cosmic', he concludes, 'neither the natural self, nor the collective mass...but a new creature' will inherit eternal life.

'The Seeing Eye' (originally titled 'Onward Christian Spacemen' by an American magazine) comes in 1963. It begins, 'The Russians [say they] have not found God in outer space'. Lewis responds that God is neither an object located in a particular place nor diffused throughout space. Expressing scepticism about the wonders of meeting other species, Lewis writes: 'I observe how the white man has hitherto treated the black, and how, even among civilized men, the stronger have treated the weaker....I do not doubt that the same story will be repeated. We shall enslave, deceive, exploit or exterminate.' His main point is this: 'if God created the universe, he created space-time, which is to the universe as the metre is to a poem, or the key is to music...more movement in space will never bring you nearer to him', since 'a fish is no more, and no less, in the sea after it has swum a thousand miles than it was when it set out'. 'Much', Lewis tells us, 'depends on the seeing eye.'

In 1958 he publishes the sly *Reflections on the Psalms*, in 1960 *The Four Loves*. The first is probably influenced by Joy (who had pointed out to Lewis some elements of humour that the non-Jew would probably miss). Reviewers seem deeply appreciative, though one allows that its connection to the Psalms is 'tenuous'. The second is based on his 'Ten Talks on Love' recorded in London 19–20 August 1958, and broadcast over American radio stations at the invitation of Caroline Rakestraw (not 'Cartwheel', as Lewis would joke) of the Episcopal Radio-TV Foundation in Georgia. The broadcasts were made in full (despite a complaint that he was too candid in his discussion of *eros*: Lewis was angered and, in effect, said all or nothing) but not transmitted over the network; each station made its own selections.

From Catholic to Protestant to secular venues the book was very well received: a 'minor classic', wrote the *New York Times*.

Reflections on the Psalms

Lewis's slyness lies in his early claim, that 'this is not what is called an "apologetic" work. I am nowhere trying to convince unbelievers that Christianity is true.' And he isn't, at least not directly. He continues, 'man can't be always defending the truth; there must be a time to feed on it'. Surely a person can both defend and feed simultaneously, as Lewis has. And just as surely persuasion can be oblique, as Lewis has shown.

Lewis's twelve chapters have names such as 'The Cursings', 'Sweeter than Honey', 'Connivance', 'Nature', 'Scripture', and 'Second Meanings in the Psalms'. His reflections include those on the psalmist as a plaintiff in civil court, glory, obedience, the dangers of an 'inner ring' that tempts to power, ordinacy, and the functioning of 'transposition', that use of a limited keyboard (so to speak) to express a reality far beyond our range of perception. In other words, Lewis's reflections on the poems (he does discuss their poetic diction and structure early on, in the context of song) becomes praise for them: for their variety of voices, lessons, dramatic surrogacy, and for the sheer thoroughness of the psychological, moral, and spiritual depths they contain.

When discussing judgement, he lessons us on our mode of quarrelling which (owing to our penchant for ranting) can become a form of blackmail. His discussion of cursings leads him to a meditation on forgiveness; not forgiving is to tempt the offender to resentment. In the chapter 'The Fair Beauty of the Lord' he cites references to the harp, lute, tambourine, and song ('a cheerful song'). But then comes the lesson. This is rowdiness, he admits, and the 'Romans, the Orthodox, and the Salvation Army all, I think, have retained more of it than we [Anglicans]. We have a terrible concern about good taste.' His last chapter offers as good a peroration (a characteristic strength) as any in his work. Melchizedek, the priest-king who comes from nowhere, who blesses in the name of the 'most high God, possessor of heaven and earth...really does point to Him'. He ends with a telling analogy. After reminding the reader how surprising time ('always the aching wound') can be, 'as though [it] were again and again a novelty', comes the clinching image:

> It is as strange as if a fish were repeatedly surprised at the wetness of water. And that would be strange indeed; unless of course the fish were destined to become, one day, a land animal.

The Four Loves

As in *Miracles*, Lewis is philosophical, examining the contours of a concept, clearing away intellectual underbrush, and diagnosing distortions. His six chapters are these: 'Introduction', in which we learn of Gift-Love and Need-Love and our nearness to God, either by likeliness or by approach; then 'Liking and Loves for the Sub-human' (e.g. for nature and for the purely local), where he discusses Need-Pleasure and Appreciative-Pleasure, urging the reader to apologize for neither. There follow the loves proper. First is 'Affection' (called Storge, natural affection, as for family); then 'Friendship' (Philia, when 'they stand together' beholding some common interest—the love most free of our nervous system and as such not strictly necessary); followed by 'Eros' (where the lovers behold each other strictly for the sake of the other: we learn that 'love ceases to be a demon when he ceases to be a god'); and finally 'Charity', or Agape, unconditional love of the sort God has for us.

A distortion of particular interest may derive from Affection, 'the humblest love'. It often mixes with other loves and broadens us, but it can lead to possessive jealousy (as with Orual: 'The girl was mine...? I was my own and Psyche was mine'). Lewis reminds us that all natural loves may be inordinate, but Affection (which is both need-love and gift-love) can be conflicted. 'We have a right to expect it. If the others do not give it, they are "unnatural"', and the excesses that result are palpable. A person devotes a whole life (without having been asked) to caring for another and feels entitled to reciprocity. Or one family member 'flashes ahead...or perhaps undergoes a religious conversion.... The other is left behind.' So the new interest is labelled silly nonsense, or the convert 'affected'.

As usual, Lewis's self-references are both telling and poignant; but his knowledge of human nature and custom evidence a man who has paid very close attention to people. (He always thought experience 'such a reliable thing', if one paid attention to it.) We know what he means when he warns, 'anything not eternal is eternally out of date'.

The Death of Joy

Lewis was busy, but busiest with family matters (see Figure 9). He was seeing to the education of Joy's sons (whom he would adopt); David (1944–2015), the eldest, would eventually attend a rabbinical college, study ancient languages, travel a good deal, visit Israel, and marry. Douglas (b. 1945) would acquire agricultural interests, eventually move to Australia, become a successful broadcaster, and raise a family with Merry, his wife. Of the two, David would have nothing to do with the Lewis 'industry', though always expressing both love for and gratitude to Lewis. (Douglas would become a gatekeeper with a proprietary interest in that industry.) For the most part they were away at school, but when Douglas is at home Lewis finds him good and cheerful company. The brothers have little to do with each other. Warren is drinking so heavily that he must be with the friendly nuns in Drogheda, Ireland.

As it happens, Joy's cancer was only in remission and her pain returns. Still, along with Roger Lancelyn Green, the Lewises travel

9. Joy Davidman Lewis and C. S. Lewis at the Kilns.

to Greece. They climb to the Acropolis, make excursions, including stops on the way home, and are happy, though Lewis finally must wheel Joy in a chair. She dies on 13 July 1960, shortly after their trip. The following epitaph that Joy requested for herself is cut in marble at the Oxford Crematorium:

Here the whole world (stars, water, air,
And field, and forest, as they were
Reflected in a single mind)
Like cast off clothes was left behind
In ashes…Reborn…
In Lenten lands, hereafter may
Resume them on her Easter Day.

Bill Gresham would visit his sons, but any bonding at this stage proved impossible. He and Lewis would get along well enough. On 14 September 1962, Gresham takes his own life.

Some corresponding friends—Sister Penelope stands out—are comforting. A year later, Lewis publishes *A Grief Observed* under the pseudonym N. W. Clerk. It would help millions who are grieving. (A number of Lewis's correspondents, not knowing the real author but knowing of Lewis's loss, would send him the book for his consolation.)

A Grief Observed

Lewis had long contemplated grief, having written *Five Sonnets* on the subject for a decade and more. Thoughts from those poems would find their way into this very short book, consisting of notes made in the aftermath of Joy's death. He variously equates grief with fear, is further saddened by his inability even to remember what Joy looked like, meditates on the healing function of marriage, and is eventually very, very angry at God. Some will think he has lost his faith. He still prays for other dead friends, 'but when I try to pray for H. [Joy was in fact Helen Joy], I halt. Bewilderment and amazement come over me. I have a ghastly sense of unreality, of speaking into a vacuum about a nonentity.'

A bit later he observes, like a Christian author who might be planning a book on pain, 'the tortures occur. If they are unnecessary, then there is no god or a bad one. If there is a good god then these tortures are necessary.' He wonders if God is a sadist. Even if the pain is for our own good, he tells those who counsel comfort, 'either way, we're for it.... Have they never even been to a dentist?'

And then, suddenly: 'I find I can believe again.... Something quite unexpected happened.... my heart was lighter than it had been for many weeks.' He realizes that when he mourned H. least, he remembered her best. The descent is over, the ascent begun; rhetorical artifice—Lewis looking at himself and, knowing he would publish this most intimate of books, at his readership too—has not compromised sincerity or truth. At the end he writes, 'she said not to me but to the chaplain, "I am at peace with God". She smiled but not at me.'

The following poem was not published during Lewis's lifetime:

> All this is flashy rhetoric about loving you.
> I never had a selfless thought since I was born.
> I am mercenary and self-seeking through and through:
> I want God, you, all friends merely to serve my turn.
> Peace, re-assurance, pleasure, are the goal I seek,
> I cannot crawl one inch outside my proper skin:
> I talk of love—a scholar's parrot may talk Greek—
> But, self-imprisoned, always end where I begin.
> Only that now you have taught me (but how late) my lack.
> I see the chasm. And everything you are was making
> My heart into a bridge by which I might get back
> From exile, and grow man. And now the bridge is breaking.
> For this I bless you as the ruin falls. The pains
> You give me are more precious than all other gains.

Chapter 7
End game

In 1945 Charles Williams arranged a meeting between his two friends, T. S. Eliot and C. S. Lewis. Given the uncongenial literary past the men shared, and Eliot's rudeness (opening with the observation that Lewis looked older in person), it did not go well. Williams was amused. In the late 1950s, however, the men met again, this time to revise the Psalter and, despite differences, warmed to each other. The Lewises and the Eliots would dine twice together, and Lewis would say that he came to love Eliot who, when *A Grief Observed* was offered pseudonymously to Faber and Faber (Eliot's editorial home), knew immediately who the author was and declared it must be published.

The same congeniality was not shared by Lewis and the 'Leavisites'. F. R. Leavis had been a Cambridge man long before Lewis arrived, and his critical approach—ferociously judgemental (or 'evaluative') and condescending—was the dominant trend. His neophiliac 'Leavisites' (angry, snobbish, take-no-prisoners followers who, in Lewis's view, mistook literature for religion) attacked Lewis, as did Leavis. Lewis responded severely, first by pointing out the vagaries of the young critics then (directly to Leavis) wondering how a mature critic could not know the difference between a disputation and a quarrel marked by name-calling. Perhaps the heart of the matter lay implicitly in a book on language Lewis had published in 1960.

A Study in Words

Lewis's purpose is to gloss certain key words etymologically and culturally so that when students read an old book they will know what the author meant. The key is 'old books', because, first, the Leavisites did not see those as relevant to a literary education and, second, believed that almost any interpretation of a book, especially one far beyond the possibility of authorial intent, was acceptable, the more extreme the better.

In his Introduction, Lewis acknowledges that language changes, often for the better, but claims that it also deteriorates. That language is best that can make distinctions, that is not inflated nor used as a substitute for hard thinking, and that is not misappropriated to express mere approval or disapproval. Such abuses he calls 'verbicide'. He goes on to describe seven 'themes' (e.g. ramification, the importance of context, the moralization of status-words) that will recur in his study of the eleven words or phrases that follow. The most important theme, I believe, is the Dangerous Sense, which is what Lewis calls a word that has shrunk (e.g. 'furniture') to mean one thing. (Now we might think of 'gay'.)

The following 290 pages treat such words as 'nature', 'wit', 'simple', 'conscience and conscious', and 'life'. In each chapter he examines the word conceptually, for a word means more than its recognizable variation. For example, 'sad' has been used in ways related to 'grave' and 'heavy' and thus to 'serious'. Literary examples abound, introduced aptly and easily. (One doubts that Lewis, like the rest of us, would have had to look them up.)

These chapters are followed by a conclusion, 'At the Fringe of Language'. Here is the rub. Though he does not mention Leavis or his school, in context certain readers would have known his target. 'The function of criticism', he writes, 'is "to get ourselves out of the way". Alas, 'to revenge ourselves is easier and more agreeable'. He claims that adverse criticism is hard to do well and often becomes 'a blow delivered in battle'. Thus, 'the desire to condemn harshly should be a danger signal', though he admits that 'continence in this matter is no doubt painful'.

Twenty years earlier in *Rehabilitations* Lewis had shown sympathy for writers who were simply out of fashion, and it was there that he published 'High and Low Brows', in which he argues that some other standard than 'high' and 'low' (or, as we might put it, popular vs literary fiction) is needed, since there exist too many instances of one sharing both the good and bad qualities of the other. His fundamental first step is always to take the work on its own terms, 'in the same spirit that the author writ', requiring that we ask what sort of work it is, that is, examining its 'quiddity'. (Thus in his discussion of the Bible he would insist that, owing to his training, he recognizes Myth, Legend, Narrative, Poetry, and Reportage when he sees it and, without at all diminishing the inerrancy of Sacred Scripture, respects the differences among them because he recognizes them.)

'High and Low Brows' would become part of a book, a great theoretical statement, and not only on the nature of literary art and criticism; long before its critical trendiness, 'reader-response' is Lewis's answer. Unfortunately, that book is so lucid in its organization, so simple in its language (there is no jargon), so insouciant in its bypassing of the theoretical *Zeitgeist* (what else is new? for Lewis is not arguing but describing), and so brief (though longer that Aristotle's *Poetics*), that to the establishment it must have seemed slight as well as slim. In fact, for these reasons and for the prescient model Lewis renders, it is brilliant. He holds no truck with schools or trends. Above all, he wants literature to be *itself* (as opposed, say, to religion or politics), and he is no snob.

An Experiment in Criticism

The entire thrust of Lewis's argument is an irony: getting ourselves out of the way is required for the purpose of self-enlargement, which is the purpose of literature. Lewis's stirring, justly famous conclusion says it best:

> My own eyes are not enough for me.... Reality, even seen through the eyes of many, is not enough. I will see what others have invented. Even the eyes of humanity are not enough. I regret that the brutes cannot write books. Very gladly would I learn what face things present to a...bee; more gladly still would I perceive the olfactory world charged with all the information and emotion it carries for a dog. Literary experience heals the wound, without undermining the privilege, of individuality. There are mass emotions which heal the wound; but they destroy the privilege.... But in reading great literature I become a thousand men and yet remain myself.... Here, as in worship, in love, in moral action, and in knowing, I transcend myself; and am never more myself than when I do.

The eleven relatively short chapters of the book move us towards understanding that passage, which encapsulates the kernel of Lewis's experiment. 'If all went ideally well,' he postulates, 'we should end by defining good literature as that which permits, invites, or even compels good reading; and bad as that which does the same for bad reading.'

Assembling the constituents of good reading, Lewis discusses receiving a book instead of using it; 'castle-building', that is, the right ('normal') and wrong ('morbid', 'egotistical') ways for readers to participate in the work; types of realism (of content and of presentation); myth; fantasy; and the consequential differences between *Logos*, something said, and *Poiema*, something made. That distinction, coming very near the middle of the book, brings us to the core of Lewis's conception of a literary object, which must be quoted nearly in full:

> One of the prime achievements in every good fiction has nothing to do with truth or philosophy [a smack to the Leavisites].... It is the triumphant adjustment of two kinds of order. On the one hand, the events... have their chronological and causal order.... On the other, all the scenes or other divisions of the work must be related to each other according to principles of design, like the masses in a picture or the passages in a symphony. Our feelings and imaginations must be led through 'taste after taste, upheld with kindliest change'. Contrasts... between the darker and the lighter, the swifter and the slower... must have something like a balance, but never too perfect a symmetry, so that the shape of the whole work will be felt as inevitable and satisfying. Yet this second order must never confuse the first.... It is very natural that when we have gone through the ordered movements which a great play or narrative excites in us—when we have danced the dance or enacted that ritual or submitted to that pattern—it should suggest to us many interesting reflections.

Later Lewis would incur the wrath of the 'vigilant critics' with a more explicit diagnosis of its pathology (with no personal attacks), and wrath it would be. On the other hand, the book was well received by most reviewers.

'Screwtape Proposes a Toast' and 'The Inner Ring'

For Lewis, the short essay—in effect Lewis working as an opinion journalist—was the form that was often best for 'what was to be said'. As with poetry and letters, he never abandoned it. His social and political opinions are sometimes encapsulated in his titles, as with 'Willing Slaves of the Welfare State', 'Delinquents in the Snow', and 'The Death of Words'. These and others are typically instructive: he observes, mines the premises of a phenomenon, then undermines that premise. Of the several score of essays, many deal with religious themes ('What Are We to Make of Jesus Christ?'), with the interaction of religion and society ('Xmas and Christmas: A Lost Chapter from Herodotus'), with social and cultural features as he saw them ('Equality', 'The Poison of Subjectivism'), or with cultural mistakes ('The Humanitarian Theory of Punishment'). Most of these show a right-leaning disposition, but inconsistently, and none is political or partisan; rather, they dig down to differences between moral and social assumptions that prevailed in the world in which Lewis was raised and some that prevailed later in his life.

'Screwtape Proposes a Toast' (1959) was invited by the *Saturday Evening Post*. In it Lewis revisits Uncle Screwtape just this once, this time at a demonic banquet honouring the Principal of the College, one Slubglob. In addressing graduates not yet posted to a 'patient' he follows the form of an oration, his (Screwtape's) purposes being to explain the relative lack of great sinners, the abundance of lesser, barely worthy, sinners (their 'very smallness and flabbiness' makes real mortal sin almost impossible), and to indicate direction: in short, the more conformity and talk of 'religion' the better.

Lewis distinguishes between Democracy, a form of governance, and democracy, a state of mind that says 'I'm as good as you' and is welcome in Hell: it discourages real merit, ridicules the source (largely the middle class) of those who contribute genuine achievements to society, and promotes dullards (who can do no more than ape popular culture, because to learn more than that is too difficult). At the bottom, of course, is Envy—a quick route to Hell. His history is hasty and his targets are too easy (I think), but these pot-shots—especially his attack on modern education—work in context. They get him to his main point, namely, that devils must aim for the destruction of individuals by encouraging the 'delusion that the fate of nations is *in itself* more important than that of individual souls'.

There are no surprises, either thematically or tonally: he was and remains a countercultural agent behind enemy lines, and the piece is representative of a certain fugitive stance and voice. The difference here is that themes repeated elsewhere are now tightly packed into one piece, with no amelioration, qualification, or even argument (but this is Uncle Screwtape, after all). Does Lewis-Screwtape overreach in his pessimism and condemnation? Perhaps, rather like an astute doctor who, with great keenness, has diagnosed a number of cancerous polyps but has mistakenly pronounced each as having metastasized.

'The Inner Ring' (an address from 1944) is quite different, in purpose, tone, and theme. It is focused. Lewis will give advice to his young audience about living (but not about current affairs), advice dealing with a single strong temptation; not a temptation to sin but one which might occasion it. 'I believe', he writes, 'that in all men's lives...one of the most dominant elements is the desire to be inside the local Ring, and the terror of being left outside'. The temptation may lead to the abandonment of real friends, to complicity in low-level vulgarities or high-level immoralities (as Lewis depicts in *That Hideous Strength*), or to betrayals and treachery that can never be undone, all for 'the delicious sense of secret intimacies' that comes with belonging to the real centre of power, that system *next to* the official system.

With his customary candour Lewis tells his audience, 'it is almost certain that at least two or three of you before you die will have become something very like scoundrels'. On the other hand, if one breaks the Ring by devotion to good work it may not put that person among 'those in the Know' but will prevent the 'periodic scandal'. Furthermore, 'if in your spare time you consort simply with the people you like, you will find that you have come unawares to a real inside'. He continues, 'this is friendship. Aristotle placed it among the virtues.' Such a band will *look* like an Inner Ring, but, in fact, because based upon genuine affection it brings 'perhaps half of all the happiness in the world, and no Inner Ring can ever have it'.

Life goes on, for a while

Owing to an enlarged prostate, diagnosed on 24 June, Lewis's
health began to fail in 1961; an operation was deemed imprudent
because Lewis's kidneys and heart were already compromised.
Warren continued to help with correspondence and to publish on
favourite figures of 17th-century France. Arthur Greeves visited
the Kilns for the last time, noting that Lewis looked ill. He would
wear a catheter, sleep sitting up, and maintain a very restricted
diet. Meanwhile, he was seeing to the boys' schooling, including
that of a troubled David, who finally found his way with rabbinical
studies; Lewis had retained for him tutors in Hebrew and Yiddish.
Once in hospital he received blood transfusions, which helped
enormously. He listened to an operatic version of *Perelandra*
and dealt with correspondence. Finally he was deemed fit enough
to return to Cambridge, from which he had been absent, but the
heavy schedule of lecturing and other projects proved taxing.

End game

Jean Wakeman, a friend of Joy's, saw the sons as frequently as
possible; Douglas became devoted to her. At one point the BBC
visited the Kilns to record Lewis's lecture on *The Pilgrim's
Progress*, and he prepared *They Asked for a Paper* for publication
(1962). A controversy over J. A. T. Robinson's *Honest to God*
broke out: apparently according to Robinson one could believe
anything or nothing. But Lewis was in no mood to engage in
sectarian polemics. He would tidy up his lectures on the
background to medieval literature (the Prolegomena he had
been delivering for decades) as a book, but owing to printing
errors publication would be delayed until after his death.

The Discarded Image

Given the scope of learning in this book, it should have been
nearly 700 pages, rather than the 230 that it is. It shows Lewis's
astonishing ability to organize material, to present it without

irrelevancies but with precisely demonstrative examples, to compare and contrast old books and worldviews with those that are current (by *enjoying* the former while *contemplating* the latter, as any living dinosaur of genius might), to bring wit to the task (the modern invention that the systematizing medieval mind would have admired is the card index), and to take delight in the 'splendour, sobriety, and coherence' of the old model which, though false, is no more false than ours, for any model is at one end of a two-way street, the other being the spirit of its age and the questions it prompts.

Six chapters, amply subdivided, address selected materials from the classical and seminal periods (e.g. Lucan, Apuleius, Boethius); the heavens; the *longaevi* ('long-livers', or daemons, who were neither human nor angelic); and Earth and its inhabitants (the longest section, with nine subdivisions, including one on the seven liberal arts). Enveloping these are chapter 1, 'The Medieval Situation', a second chapter on 'Reservations' (really a primer on thinking), and the last, 'The Influence of the Model'. These are followed by an Epilogue.

To summarize this book would be to repeat it, such is its concision. The reader comes away with the picture in mind, one marked by confidence in authority, hierarchy (especially heavenly), hard-won learning, anonymity (writers did not claim originality), knowledge (not only of influences but the workings of influence), some appreciation of the contributions of great minds (e.g. Cicero, 1st century BC; Macrobius, 5th century), and bits of fact that surprise. Medieval people knew the cosmos was grandly scaled, that the Earth was round, and that if it was at the centre it is because we matter least not most: we are small and inert compared to the heavens beyond. Those are populated, so that to gaze up is to look in, not out. We learn that within the orbit of the Moon mutability reigns but that beyond that things are 'fixed'. The model is religious (God moves the *Primum Mobile* that moves the seven crystalline, spherical heavens) but not Christian. All this, and very much more.

Scholars who reviewed the book were lavish in their praise. Dame Helen Gardner wrote, 'nobody else could have imposed such form on such a mass of matter...a book so wide in scope and implication...discovering the rare, the remote, but the exact, example. And where else...can we find so generous and enthusiastic a temper?' In his penultimate paragraph, Lewis plants his anti-Leavisite flag for the last time, displaying the same reversed perspective that is his hallmark: 'Literature exists to teach what is useful, to honour what deserves honour, to appreciate what is delightful. The useful, honourable, and delightful things are superior to it: it exists for their sake; its own use, honour, or delightfulness is derivative from theirs.'

'Men must endure their going hence'

Finally his ill health forced his resignation. On 15 June 1963, he suffered a heart attack. At one point back in hospital he went into a coma. Upon recovering he recognized Maureen (Moore) Blake, who stated her name. Lewis corrected her, saying she is Lady Dunbar, and when she asked how he could remember that he answered, 'how could *I* forget a fairy tale?' After brief bouts of in-and-out consciousness, he recovered and went home.

This final stage of Lewis's life is brief and not nearly as melancholic as some sources suggest. He did not fear death (thinking Lazarus the first martyr because he was brought back). As friends visited he continued to enjoy a version of the life he had had in the early 1950s, and he considered proposing marriage to the poet Ruth Pitter, whom he apparently decided not to burden with his own failing health. The local vicar administered the sacrament to him on Wednesdays. His caregiver, Alec Ross, helped. He had invited an American visitor, Walter Hooper, to be his secretary, but after a few weeks Hooper had to return to teaching duties in the United States.

When he returned soon after Lewis's death the trustees of Lewis's estate invited him to stay on and edit Lewis's works. Some twenty years later there irrupted an accusation that Hooper had forged at least one Lewis work (the fragment known as *The Dark Tower*). That accusation evolved into a febrile personal attack on Hooper by a small number of factionalists. In the event, the many people looking into the matter found no foundation to the charges, which were finally put to rest when a former Lewis pupil, the distinguished scholar Alastair Fowler (who edited Lewis's *Spenser's Images of Life*), revealed that he had seen the *Tower* manuscript at least a decade before Hooper came on the scene. In 2009 Hooper was given the prestigious Clyde S. Kilby Lifetime Achievement Award by the Wade Center of Wheaton College, by far the most important repository of Lewis works and papers.

In a letter to Sister Penelope, Lewis wonders if 'prison visiting' is allowed, that she might come down 'and look me up in Purgatory'. To his Cambridge friend Richard Ladborough he wrote a card inviting his colleague to dinner, adding that he was reading the notorious *Les Liaisons Dangereuses*, 'wow what a book!' In October Warren wrote, 'the wheel had come full circle. Again we were in the new "little end room", shutting out from our talk the ever present knowledge that the holidays were ending, a new term fraught with unknown possibilities awaited us both.' Jack died at home on 22 November 1963, the same day as JFK's murder. The world would learn of this days later; only sixteen friends attended the funeral. Warren, incapacitated, was not among them. Later, though, he would write, 'At five-thirty I heard a crash in his bedroom, and running in I found him lying unconscious at the foot of his bed. He ceased to breathe some three or four minutes later.' The last book he would see through the press, *Letters to Malcolm, Chiefly on Prayer*, would be published shortly after his death. (We will consider it in Chapter 8.)

Among those at his funeral was Peter Bayley, who wrote, 'there was one candle on the coffin as it was carried out into the

10. The Lewis plaque in Westminster Abbey.

churchyard. It seemed not only appropriate but almost a symbol of the man and his integrity and his absoluteness and his faith that the flame burned so steadily, even in the open air, and seemed so bright, even in the bright sun' (Figure 10).

Box 3 A selection of Lewis's critics

'Critics' here refers to those who attacked Lewis's apologetic project, or a big part of it, more or less wholesale, or Lewis personally, not to those who argued against Lewisian positions.

1. Beversluis, John. *C. S. Lewis and the Search for Rational Religion*, 1985. A reasonable questioning of Lewis's apologetic programme by a former Christian. Especially noteworthy for its rejection of Lewis's claim, in *A Grief Observed* that he (Lewis) never lost his faith. An intellectually engaging book that has merited its rejoinders.

2. Holbrook, David. 'The Problem of C. S. Lewis', *Children's Literature in Education*, no. 10 (March 1973): 3–25. This attack is close to an *ad hominem* rant. *The Chronicles* express Lewis's psychic hunger for his dead, all-bad 'castrating mother'. The children never escape determinism; and hate and sadism are unrelieved. Easily the most hostile attack on *The Chronicles* and on Lewis.

3. Haldane, J. B. S. 'Auld Hornie, F. R. S.', *Modern Quarterly*, N.S., vol. 1, no. 4 (Autumn 1946). (See Lewis's 'A Reply to Professor Haldane in *Of Other Worlds*', ed. Walter Hooper.) Haldane attacks the Ransom Trilogy as anti-science and anti-scientist and claims its science is false. Lewis's reply (neglected by Lewis scholars and readers alike) smoothly displays his learning (and Haldane's literary and historical ignorance) and is a major statement of his beliefs and methods.

4. Hynes, Samuel. 'Guardian of the Old Ways', *New York Times Book Review*, 8 July 1979. Hynes shows his own bigotries in this review of *C. S. Lewis at the Breakfast Table*, e.g. pro-nuclear disarmament, pro-Modernist, anti-Christian. Hynes does not like Lewis or the 'regular' life he lived. Some of Hynes's claims

are contradicted by testimony from contributors to the collection.

5. Miller, Laura. *The Magician's Book: A Skeptic's Adventures in Narnia*, 2008. Miller lives up to her subtitle with breadth and equanimity. At times old fashioned (it's late in the day to be quoting Freud for support), argumentatively flimsy (to charge 'racism' one is obligated to define 'racism'), or simply mistaken (Hooper is not a Catholic priest), Miller's fluent writing brings conviction to a rich personal statement.

6. Nott, Kathleen. *The Emperor's Clothes*, 1953. A broadside that attacks Lewis as vulgar, coarse, and a 'fundamentalist' who gives small importance to joy—a remarkably ignorant assertion. Her belligerence reveals a partisan to whom rational argument is unfamiliar.

7. Pittinger, Norman. 'A Critique of C. S. Lewis', *Christian Century*, vol. 75 (1 October 1958), pp. 1104–7. See Lewis's 'Rejoinder to Dr. Pittinger', *The Christian Century*, vol. 65 (26 November 1958), pp. 1359–61 and in *God in the Dock*. A debate between two Christians, one liberalizing the other not. Pittinger is impatient with Lewis's level of discourse, thinking it simplistic. Lewis's response is that he is 'writing *ad populum*, not *ad clerum*' (i.e. for laypeople not professionals).

8. Pullman, Phillip. *His Dark Materials*, trilogy, 1995, 1997, 2000. Pullman is on the side of Milton's Satan, happy at his rebellion and its consequence for the human race. *The Chronicles* are 'blatantly racist', 'monumentally disparaging of women', 'immoral', and 'evil'. He is a man with a mission. He is a very fine writer, though some readers have found the trilogy running out of steam in the middle of the second book.

Chapter 8
The weight of glory

Responses to Lewis

His critics have often railed against him (see Box 3). In his *Language and Silence* George Steiner called him 'the enemy' (representing 'coziness, frivolity, mundane cliques'), and R. C. Churchill (in 'Mr. C. S. Lewis as an Evangelist') is harsh in his denunciation (for example, Lewis has used 'the church as an excuse for his dreary attacks on everything he hasn't bothered to understand... Liberalism, Humanitarianism, the Life-Force, Modern Art'). Even some of his Christian colleagues found his apologetic militancy unpalatable. Dorothy L. Sayers—novelist, translator of Dante, fellow defender of the faith, and Lewis's friend—had her reservations: 'One trouble... is his fervent missionary zeal... He is apt to think that one should rush into every fray and strike a blow for Christendom, whether or not one is equipped.'

Conversely, distinguished scholars such as Dame Helen Gardner and Louis Bredvold have written highly of him; reviewers such as Edmund Fuller have praised his work; literary artists and journalists have cited him for his authority and breadth, and ordinary readers have found still other sources of his appeal. Fifty years ago members of the New York C. S. Lewis Society identified some sources of his appeal, intangible characteristics of style or voice, which seem as much a part of the man as any doctrine. *Brilliance, clarity, Britishness, nobility, humility, veracity,* and *joy* were the words used by the membership. Those who met Lewis personally have remarked upon these same qualities. As Thomas Howard (scholar and critic) put it, he was 'down to the last molecule the man I would have expected'.

Lewis's appeal

A general strategy, remarkably, is that he never *directly* argues in defence of a doctrine, not even the Incarnation. Debra Winger, who played Joy in the movie *Shadowlands*, has touched on this crucial aspect of Lewis's appeal:

> He [makes] difficult questions accessible. I don't think he makes the answers 'easy'. I don't think he answers questions. I think he discusses them. He's in that school of discourse where his statements are not like books that are written by experts. He's saying 'think about this'. That's why I think he opened Christianity to so many people.

That stylistic pattern is almost ubiquitous in his work. He takes the reader from the *possible* to the *plausible* to the intensely *pleasurable* to the *promising* and thence to the glories of *hope* (thus the many anthologies). Here Lewis's poem 'Reason' might be applied to Lewis himself:

> Who [will] make imagination's dim exploring touch
> Ever report the same as intellectual sight?
> Then could I truly say, and not deceive,
> Then wholly say, that I BELIEVE.

And yet he was not always casting spells. Consider the following, one of his most famous arguments, from *Mere Christianity*, about the divinity of Jesus:

> A man who was merely a man and said the sort of things Jesus said would not be a great moral teacher. He would either be a lunatic—on

The weight of glory

109

the level with the man who says he is a poached egg—or else he would be the Devil of Hell. You must make your choice. Either this man was, and is, the Son of God, or else a madman or something worse. You can shut him up for a fool, you can spit at him and kill him as a demon or you can fall at his feet and call him Lord and God, but let us not come with any patronizing nonsense about his being a great human teacher. He has not left that open to us. He did not intend to.

The severity of both logic and tone are striking.

Logic and tone; genre, sensibility, learning; honesty, humility, orthodoxy; stylistic dexterity: no one feature can explain the effectiveness of Lewis's body of work. The closest anyone has come, I believe, is Paul Holmer, in his *C. S. Lewis, the Shape of His Faith and Thought*:

> He shows us repeatedly…how a kind of moral certitude is finally achieved. He sends us back to our fathers, mothers, nurses, poets, sages, and lawgivers. The dignity he ascribes to all of us is exceedingly flattering.…The tissue of life around us, when taken with seriousness, is already a moral order. We have to become its qualified readers.…The world has no single character, and it must be understood in a variety of ways. His books create…the living variety of paradigms.…For his works, especially the novels, have a way of creating a kind of longing for innocence, for purity, for humility, candor, and contentment.…Only its occasion can be created by another, and that is what Lewis's literature becomes. Wisdom has to be read off the whole shape of his thought and is not one trick within it.

Adding to that is Eugene McGovern, a founding member of the New York C. S. Lewis Society, who in his 'Our Need for Such a Guide' wrote that for Lewis 'the center remained unchanged'.

St Augustine taught the apologist to instruct, to sway, and, by variations of style, to 'subdue the will' of the audience. Above all, however, he insists that 'the man whose life is in harmony with his teaching will teach with greater effect'. Closer to home, Richard Cunningham ends his *C. S. Lewis: Defender of the Faith* with the same observation: 'When the idea of not-God and the idea of Lewis meet in a sympathetic mind, it is the idea of not-God that must change. Lewis himself is his finest Christian apology.'

Hope

The novelist and philosopher Walker Percy provides a view that fittingly describes what Lewis has accomplished:

> What man is cannot be grasped by the science of man. The case is rather that man's science is one of the things that man does, a mode of existence....Man is not merely a higher organism responding to and controlling his environment. He is...that being in the world whose calling it is to find a name for Being, to give testimony to it, and to provide for it a clearing.

That is, Hope, which points to ultimate meaning.

That is why, of the many biblical verses that express this heart of Lewisian thinking, the most evocative is Hebrews 6:19–20: 'I will shower blessings upon you...we now have found safety... encouragement to take a firm grip on the hope that is held out to us. Here we have an anchor for our soul as sure as it is firm and reaching right through beyond the veil where Jesus entered before us and on our behalf.' Two items seem to be a gloss on that passage. I have saved them for this final chapter because they are seminal, expressing best the heart of Lewis's project, and among the most moving pieces that he ever wrote. This first is an essay that appeared in *Religion in Life* in 1953; the second is Lewis's greatest sermon—indeed, perhaps his greatest religious statement.

In 'The World's Last Night' Lewis once again (as with the presence of pain, or with glossolalia, or with the efficacy of prayer) takes

The weight of glory

on a difficult item, Jesus's promise of His Second Coming. How challenging is it? Given the promises—as yet unfulfilled—Lewis insists we cannot marginalize it; in fact, 'if this is not an integral part of the faith', he says, 'I do not know what is'. Lewis poses the challenge candidly: the claim is the 'most embarrassing verse in the bible'. Then he reminds us of what comes next: 'But of that day and that hour knoweth no man... not the angels... neither the Son, but the Father.'

Our mistake is to try to guess where we are in the story, which act, and to predict our place in it. But our perspective is mistaken, and, typically, Lewis corrects it with an example. In *King Lear*, a man with a mere eight lines seeks to defend Gloucester by threatening his own master at sword point. He is killed and gone, but, says Lewis, in real life *that* is the role you would want. That is why we must take to heart John Donne's question: 'What if this present were the world's last night?' For the end will also be a judgement, one under another light than our own:

> Women sometimes have the problem of trying to judge by artificial light how a dress will look by daylight. That is very like the problem of all of us: to dress our souls not for the electric lights... but for the daylight of the next. The good dress is the one that will face that light. For that light will last longer.

'The Weight of Glory' was preached in the Church of St Mary the Virgin in Oxford on 8 June 1941. His subject is longing, the core of his conversion and of much of his writing. The simple argument is that if nothing here satisfies this longing then we are made for elsewhere. Certainly he knows that this feeling has been attacked as adolescence or nostalgia, and he knows that merely discussing it can be embarrassing. So he asks, 'do you think I am trying to weave a spell? Perhaps I am; but remember your fairy tales. Spells are used for breaking enchantments [too]... to wake us from the evil enchantment of worldliness.'

Just as hunger proves there must be such a thing as food, so this longing leads to Heaven. But what does Heaven offer? Here Lewis surveys the promises of scripture, the importance of which turn on biblical images of glory suggesting either fame or luminosity. The first, he says, is a competitive passion; as for the second, 'who wishes to become a kind of living electric light bulb?' Yet this promise of glory makes for 'a weight or burden of glory which our thoughts can hardly sustain'. Now, alas, we are outside trying to look into that of which beauty, grace, and the power of nature are images. But 'all the leaves of the New Testament are rustling with the rumour that it will not always be so. Some day, God willing, we shall get in.'

Lewis's peroration here is perhaps his greatest. The weight of my neighbour's glory 'should be laid daily on my back', for 'there are no *ordinary* people. You have never talked to a mere mortal. Nations, cultures, arts, civilization—these are mortal, and their life is to ours as the life of a gnat. But it is immortal…horrors or everlasting splendours' that 'we joke with, marry, snub, or exploit'.

I know of no one who has been called a 'Lewisite'; nor is there any such thing as 'Lewisism'. Rather, instead of being of a school or professing a theory, his body of work is as he described that of Edmund Spenser, whose poetry he cherished: 'a growing thing, a tree…with branches to heaven and roots to hell.…And between these two extremes comes all the multiplicity of human life.…To read him is to grow in mental health.' When brilliance of expression, intellectual authority, and breadth of achievement; reliability, reason, reasonableness, and the promise of glory all cohere, the allure is commonly irresistible.

Letters to Malcolm, Chiefly on Prayer

Shortly after Lewis's death the last book he saw through the press, *Letters to Malcolm, Chiefly on Prayer*, was published. Like others (*Reflections on the Psalms*, *A Grief Observed*) it is oblique: the letters are not actual, there is no Malcolm. The rhetorical device allows for intimacy, the reader 'overhearing' apparently unsystematic thinking expressed in a secure setting: the real man at ease, his voice resolved, its music tender. It is a meditation on prayer and praying, with praying the Lord's Prayer as an extended personal example.

Lewis had made false starts at the book in 1952 and 1954; in 1963 the idea of feigned correspondence (again) came to him, and in two months he was done. He insists that he is not teaching and that his subject is personal prayer only. To this end he invented not only Malcolm but Malcolm's wife Betty and his son George; references to them (the book ends with 'thank Betty for her note') enhance the relaxed intimacy of tone, one of comparing notes. In Letter XII he allows that 'my experience is the same as yours. I have never met a book on prayer which was much use to people in our position.' His book would prove the exception.

There are lessons, of course, but these seem more like tips, his way of once again 'sneaking past those watchful dragons'. He prefers 'home-made' prayers but needs ready-made ones to stay in touch with doctrine. He will pray *with* the saints and *for* the dead. We must 'unveil' ourselves. He is fond of 'festooning', that is, glossing a line from, say, the Lord's Prayer: 'Thy will be done'—by me now, that sort of thing. Petitionary prayer (as when, for example, 'George' becomes ill) can be Christ-like: in Gethsemane He asked His father to spare Him. In asking God for something, Lewis believes, we know we may be refused but we also know that we were heard; God's providence is always special rather than rule-governed. Thus prayer shows 'events are . . . created like a work of art'.

In Letter XIX he discusses Holy Communion. The theological thickets (e.g. 'accident' vs 'substance') are side-stepped: 'The command, after all, was Take, eat: not Take, understand.' In discussing Purgatory, he opts for Dante's purgative view, or Newman's 'Dream of Gerontius', in which the soul begs to be cleansed. His more homely image is that of a patient coming around in the dentist's chair and having to rinse: that rinsing may be Purgatory.

The sceptical reader wants to agree, of course; that reader is no atheist. But agree or not, the following should be beyond dispute, that Lewis had a broad existential streak: not that he was irrational but, in trusting experience, that he could be non-rational. His resemblance to Kierkegaard, the godfather of Existentialism, is telling. In 'Three Kinds of Men' (1943) his analysis closely mimics that of Kierkegaard's aesthetic, ethical, and religious stages; the same is true of his frequent dependence on 'indirect communication'; and Kierkegaard's 'leap of faith' was essentially Lewis's. His response to Joy is nothing if not that.

That is why, I think, that his descriptions of his own landmark decision-making—to atheism and back again—are hardly convincing, not because they are false but because those descriptions are all he could fathom *rationally*, that is, by *contemplation*. (And that is why these two questions—'Why was he an atheist?' and 'Why did he convert?'—remain abidingly difficult to answer.) Keats was right. 'A man's life of any worth is a continual allegory—and very few eyes can see the mystery of life—a life like the Scriptures, figurative.'

Lewis's final theological thought comes at the very end of *Malcolm*. As well as anything he wrote it sums up the core of his apologetic project, the centrality of hope (which we had seen as early as *Dymer*):

> I don't say the resurrection of this body will happen at once. It may
> well be that this part of us sleeps in death, and the intellectual soul
> is sent to Lenten lands where she fasts in naked spirituality—a

ghost-like and imperfectly human condition.... Then the new earth and sky [not unlike the New Narnia emerging at the end of *The Last Battle*], the same yet not the same as these, will rise in us as we have risen in Christ. And once again... the birds will sing and the waters flow, and lights and shadows move across the hills, and the faces of our friends laugh upon us with amazed recognition. Guesses, of course, only guesses. If they are not true, something better will be.

Perhaps the best summary of Lewis's temperament comes from verses 1–6 of the third chapter of St James's Letter:

> the tongue is a small member and yet has great pretensions.
> Consider how small a fire can set a huge forest ablaze. The tongue is also a fire.

If the forests are minds and hearts, that certainly was Lewis. But as for his broad appeal as thinker, apologist, conversationalist, and scholar, Matthew Arnold, in *Culture and Anarchy*, draws a distinction between two fundamental impulses in Western culture, the Hellenic and the Hebraic, that seems like a final judgement of Lewis's work. Arnold defines the two cultures this way: 'The uppermost idea with Hellenism is to see things as they really are; the uppermost idea with Hebraism is with conduct and obedience'. Add breathtaking powers of varied expression and a genius of the will and there we have C. S. Lewis.

References

Secondary sources of quotations longer than a few words, as well as short quotations from Lewis, are listed sequentially within each chapter. Lewis sources that are discussed and cited within a chapter and that provide long quotations are not. (Complete information for secondary sources is listed in the further reading.)

Chapter 1: Lewis on the way

Brothers and Friends: The Diaries of Major Warren Hamilton Lewis.
Owen Barfield, *On C. S. Lewis.*
James Como, ed., *C. S. Lewis at the Breakfast Table and Other Reminiscences.*
Edmund Fuller, 'Christian Spaceman: C. S. Lewis', *Horizon.*
Roger Lancelyn Green and Walter Hooper, *C. S. Lewis: A Biography* (revised edition).
J. B. Phillips, *Ring of Truth: A Translator's Testimony.*

Chapter 2: Roots

Green and Hooper.
C. S. Lewis, *Surprised by Joy.*
C. S. Lewis, *Boxen* (1985).
Christopher Derrick, *C. S. Lewis and the Church of Rome.*
C. S. Lewis, *Collected Letters.*

Chapter 3: Lewis ascendant

Collected Letters.
George Sayer, *Jack: C. S. Lewis and His Times.*
C. S. Lewis at the Breakfast Table and Other Reminiscences.
Owen Barfield, *On C. S. Lewis.*
Rudolph Otto, *The Idea of the Holy.*
Don King, *C. S. Lewis, Poet.*
Neville Coghill, *Light on C. S. Lewis.*

Chapter 4: Fame

Collected Letters.
C. S. Lewis, *Mere Christianity.*
Green and Hooper.
C. S. Lewis, *Essays Presented to Charles Williams.*
C. S. Lewis, 'On Stories', *Of Other Worlds: Essays and Stories.*

Chapter 5: Darkness and light

C. S. Lewis, *Poems.*
C. S. Lewis, *George MacDonald, an Anthology.*
C. S. Lewis at the Breakfast Table and Other Reminiscences.
C. S. Lewis, *Letters: C. S. Lewis, Don Giovanni Calabria.*
Jeffrey D. Schultz and John G. West, Jr., eds, *The C. S. Lewis Readers' Encyclopedia.*
Walter Hooper, *C. S. Lewis: A Companion and Guide.*
Green and Hooper.
George MacDonald, *A Dish of Orts.*
G. K. Chesterton, 'Education in Fairy Tales'.
Kenneth Grahame, *Pagan Papers.*

Chapter 6: A new day

Poems.
Collected Letters.
C. S. Lewis, *Image and Imagination: Essays and Reviews.*
C. S. Lewis: A Companion and Guide.
C. S. Lewis, *Reflections on the Psalms.*

Abigail Santamaria, *Joy: Poet, Seeker, and the Woman Who Captivated C. S. Lewis.*
Poems.

Chapter 7: End game

Green and Hooper.
C. S. Lewis, *All My Road Before Me: The Diary of C. S. Lewis, 1922–1927.*
W. H. Lewis, *Brothers and Friends: The Diaries of Warren Hamilton Lewis.*
C. S. Lewis at the Breakfast Table and Other Reminiscences.

Chapter 8: The weight of glory

CSL: The Bulletin of the C. S. Lewis Society.
James Como, *Branches to Heaven: The Geniuses of C. S. Lewis.*
Paul Holmer, *C. S. Lewis: The Shape of His Faith and Thought.*
Poems.
Walker Percy, *The Message in the Bottle.*

Further reading

A selected readers' list of C. S. Lewis's works by type

This list is intended for use by both serious and casual readers, as well as by students. Dates indicate first publication; titles are listed chronologically within type. There are now many different publishers—and in some case, editions—of Lewis works, most easily located online.

Fictions

Sui generis (Christian)
Pilgrim's Regress (spiritual allegory: 1933).
The Screwtape Letters (satirical fantasy: 1942).
The Great Divorce (dream vision: 1946).

The Space (or Ransom) Trilogy: science fiction, or 'romances' ('epic fantasy')
Out of the Silent Planet (1938).
Perelandra (1943).
That Hideous Strength (1945).

***The Chronicles of Narnia*: children's fantasy**
The Lion, the Witch and the Wardrobe (1950).
Prince Caspian (1951).
The Voyage of the 'Dawn Treader' (1952).
The Silver Chair (1953).

The Horse and His Boy (1954).
The Magician's Nephew (1955).
The Last Battle (1956).

Novel

Till We Have Faces (1956).

Poetry

Narrative Poems (1969).
Poems (1994).

The personal Lewis

Surprised by Joy: The Shape of My Early Life (1955).
Brothers and Friends: The Diaries of Major Warren Hamilton Lewis (1982).
A Grief Observed (1961).
All My Road Before Me: The Diary of C. S. Lewis, 1922–1927 (1991).
The Collected Letters of C. S. Lewis (3 vols: 2000, 2004, 2006).

The 'occasional' Lewis: essays, sermons, reviews

Caveat: the contents of many of these books overlap. The complete collection in this category is the Essay Collection (2 vols): *Faith, Christianity and the Church* (2000) and *Literature, Philosophy and Short Stories* (2000), both edited (with original dates and venues and of republication, if applicable) by Lesley Walmsley. These can be hard to come by and very costly.

Selected and edited by Lewis himself

Transposition and Other Address (The Weight of Glory) (1949).
The World's Last Night (1960).
They Asked for a Paper (1962).

Edited by Walter Hooper

Of Other Worlds: Essays and Stories (1966).
Christian Reflections (1967).
God in the Dock (1970).
Present Concerns (1986).
Image and Imagination: Essays and Reviews (2013).

Literary history, criticism, and theory; moral philosophy*

The Allegory of Love (1936).
The Personal Heresy (1939).
Rehabilitations (1939).
A Preface to 'Paradise Lost' (1942).
The Abolition of Man (1943).*
English Literature in the Sixteenth Century, Excluding Drama (1954).
Studies in Words (1960).
An Experiment in Criticism (1961).
The Discarded Image (1964).

Christian apologetics and religious philosophy

The Problem of Pain (1940).
The Screwtape Letters (1942).
The Great Divorce (1946).
Miracles (1947).
Mere Christianity (1952).
Reflections on the Psalms (1958).
The Four Loves (1960).
Letters to Malcolm, Chiefly on Prayer (1964).
Several anthologies of Lewis quotations exist, by far the most useful being *The Quotable Lewis, an Encyclopedic Selection of Quotations from the Complete Published Works of C. S. Lewis*, edited by Wayne Martindale and Jerry Root.

Books of particular importance to C. S. Lewis

This list could include many more titles and be distributed differently, but thirty titles in four groups seems sensible.

Intellectual

Samuel Alexander, *Space, Time and Deity* (see, e.g., 'Meditation in a Toolshed').
Aristotle, *Metaphysics, Ethics*.
Owen Barfield, *Poetic Diction, History in English Words*, etc.
Edwyn Bevan, *Symbolism and Belief*.
Plato, *The Republic*.

Imaginative

Geoffrey Chaucer, *Troilus and Criseyde* (see Lewis's discussion in *The Allegory of Love*).

Dante, *The Divine Comedy*.

H. M. A. Guerber, *Myths of the Norsemen from the Eddas and Sagas*.

Homer, *The Iliad* ('This is war,' Lewis said when he arrived at the front, 'this is what Homer wrote about').

David Lindsay, *A Voyage to Arcturus*.

William Wadsworth Longfellow, 'Tegners's Drapa' in *The Seaside and the Fireside*.

William Morris, *The Well at the World's End*, *The Wood Beyond the World*.

Beatrix Potter, *Squirrel Nutkin* (especially for 'the idea of Autumn').

Edmund Spenser, *The Faerie Queene* (see Lewis's discussion in *The Allegory of Love* and *Spenser's Images of Life*, ed. Alastair Fowler).

J. R. R. Tolkien, *The Hobbit*, *The Lord of the Rings*.

Virgil, *The Aeneid* (see a partial translation by Lewis in A. T. Reyes, ed., *C. S. Lewis's Lost 'Aeneid'*).

Charles Williams, *The Place of the Lion*, etc.

Spiritual

Richard Baxter, *Church-History of the Government of Bishops* (source of 'Mere Christianity'), *The Saint's Everlasting Rest*.

Jacob Boehme, *The Way to Christ*.

G. K. Chesterton, *The Everlasting Man*.

Richard Hooker, *The Laws of Ecclesiastical Polity*.

William Law, *A Serious Call to a Devout and Holy Life*.

George MacDonald, *Phantastes*, etc. (see Lewis's *George MacDonald: an Anthology*).

Rudolph Otto, *The Idea of the Holy*.

St. Francis de Sales, *Introduction to the Devout Life*.

William Wordsworth, *The Prelude*.

Fictional

E. R. Eddison, *The Worm Ouroboros*.

Kenneth Grahame, *The Wind in the Willows*.

David Lindsay, *A Voyage to Arcturus*.

Mervyn Peake, *The Gormenghast Trilogy*.

Selected secondary sources

Adey, Lionel. *C. S. Lewis's 'Great War' with Owen Barfield* (English Literary Studies, No. 14, University of Victoria, 1978).

Barfield, Owen. *On C. S. Lewis*, ed. G. B. Tennyson (Middletown, Wesleyan University Press, 1989).

Barkman, Adam. *C. S. Lewis and Philosophy as a Way of Life* (Zossima Press, 2008).

Beversluis, John. *C. S. Lewis and the Search for Rational Religion* (Grand Rapids, Wm. B. Eerdmans, 1985).

Bredvold, Louis I. 'The Achievement of C. S. Lewis', The Intercollegiate Review, vol. 4 nos. 2–3, January–March, 1968.

Carnell, Corbin Scott. *Bright Shadows of Reality: C. S. Lewis and the Feeling Intellect* (Grand Rapids, Wm. B. Eerdmans, 1974).

Caughey, Shanna. *Revisiting Narnia: Fantasy, Myth and Religion in C. S. Lewis' Chronicles* (Dallas, BenBella Books, 2005).

Christopher, Joe R. and Joan Ostling. *C. S. Lewis: An Annotated Checklist of Writings About Him* (Kent, The Kent State University Press, 1973).

Como, James. *Branches to Heaven: The Geniuses of C. S. Lewis* (Dallas, Spence Publishing Co., 1998).

Como, James. *Remembering C. S. Lewis: Recollections of Those Who Knew Him* (San Francisco, Ignatius Press, 2005). Formerly *C. S. Lewis at the Breakfast Table and Other Reminiscences*.

Cunningham, Richard B. *C. S. Lewis: Defender of the Faith* (Philadelphia, Westminster Press, 1967).

Downing, David. *Into the Region of Awe: Mysticism in C. S .Lewis* (Downers Grove, Inter Varsity Press, 2005).

Duriez, Colin. *The Oxford Inklings: Lewis, Tolkien and Their Circle* (Oxford, Lion Hudson Books, 2015).

Edwards, Bruce. *C. S. Lewis: Life, Works, and Legacy*, four volumes (Westport, Preager Perspectives, 2007).

Ford, Paul F. *Companion to Narnia* (San Francisco, Harper & Row, 1980).

Fuller, Edmund. 'Christian Spaceman: C. S. Lewis', *Horizon*, May 1959.

Gardner, Dame Helen Louise. *Clive Staples Lewis: 1898–1963* (Oxford University Press, 1966).

Gibb, Jocelyn, ed. *Light on C. S. Lewis* (New York, Harcourt, Brace & World, Inc., 1965).

Gilchrist, K. J. *A Morning After War: C. S. Lewis and WWI* (New York, Peter Lang Publishing, Inc., 2005).

Glyer, Diana Pavlac. *The Company They Keep: C. S. Lewis and J. R. R. Tolkien as Writers in Community* (Kent, The Kent State University Press, 2007).

Goffar, Janine. *C. S. Lewis Index: Rumors from the Sculptor's Shop* (Riverside, La Sierra University Press, 1995).

Graham, David, ed. *We Remember C. S. Lewis* (Nashville, Broadman & Holman, 2001).

Green, Roger Lancelyn. *C. S. Lewis* (New York, Henry Z. Walck, Inc., 1963).

Green, Roger Lancelyn and Walter Hooper, *C. S. Lewis: A Biography*, fully revised and updated edition (London, HarperCollins, 2002).

Gresham, Douglas. *Lenten Lands: My Childhood with Joy Davidman and C. S. Lewis* (New York, Macmillan Publishing Co., 1988).

Hannay, Margaret. *C. S. Lewis* (New York, Frederick Ungar Publishing Co., 1981).

Holmer, Paul. *C. S. Lewis: The Shape of His Faith and Thought* (New York, Harper & Row, 1976).

Hooper, Walter. *Past Watchful Dragons: The Narnia Chronicles of C. S. Lewis* (London, Collier Macmillan Publishers, 1979).

Hooper, Walter. *C. S. Lewis: A Companion & Guide* (London, HarperCollins, 1996).

Howard, Thomas. *C. S. Lewis: Man of Letters* (San Francisco, Ignatius Press, 1987).

Huttar, Charles, ed. *Imagination and the Spirit* (Grand Rapids, Wm G. Eerdmans, 1971).

Keefe, Carolyn. *C. S. Lewis: Speaker and Teacher* (Grand Rapids, Zondervan, 1971).

Kilby, Clyde, ed. *An Anthology of C. S. Lewis: A Mind Awake* (New York, Harcourt Brace Jovanovich, 1968).

King, Don W. *C. S. Lewis, Poet* (Kent, The Kent State University Press, 2001).

Kreeft, Peter. *Is Your Lord Large Enough? How C. S. Lewis Expands Our View of God* (Downers Grove, InterVarsity Press, 2008).

Latta, Corey. *C. S. Lewis and the Art of Writing* (Eugene, Cascade Books, 2016).

Lawlor, John. *C. S. Lewis: Memories and Reflections* (Dallas, Spence Publishing Co., 1998).

Lindskoog, Kathryn. *C. S. Lewis: Mere Christian* (Downers Grove, InterVarsity Press, 1981).

Lowenberg, Susan. *C. S. Lewis: A Reference Guide, 1972–1988* (New York, G. K. Hall & Co., 1993).

McGovern, Eugene. 'C. S. Lewis,' *Dictionary of Literary Biography, vol. 15: British Novelists* (Farmington Hills, Gale Publishers, 1983).

McGrath, Alister. *C. S. Lewis: A Life* (Carol Stream, Tyndale House Publishers, 2012).

Manlove, Colin. *C. S. Lewis: His Literary Achievement* (Cheshire, Winged Lion Press, 2010.

Markos, Louis. *Lewis Agonistes* (Nashville, Broadman & Holman Publishers, 2003).

Martindale, Wayne and Jerry Root, eds. *The Quotable C. S. Lewis* (Wheaton, Tyndale House Publishers, 1990).

Meilander, Gilbert. *The Taste for the Other: The Social and Ethical Thought of C. S. Lewis* (Grand Rapids, Wm. B. Eerdmans, 1978).

Mills, David, ed. *The Pilgrim's Guide: C. S. Lewis and the Art of Witness* (Grand Rapids, Wm. B. Eerdmans, 1998).

Myers, Doris T. *C. S. Lewis in Context* (Kent, The Kent State University Press, 1994).

Nicholi, Armand M., Jr. *The Question of God: C. S. Lewis and Sigmund Freud Debate God, Love, Sex, and the Meaning of Life* (New York, The Free Press, 2002).

Phillips, Justin. *C. S. Lewis in a Time of War* (San Francisco, HarperCollins, 2002).

Santamaria, Abigail. *Joy: Poet, Seeker, and the Woman Who Captivated C. S. Lewis* (Boston, Houghton Mifflin Harcourt, 2015).

Sayer, George. *Jack: C. S. Lewis and His Times* (San Francisco, Harper & Row, 1988).

Schakel, Peter J. *Reading With The Heart: The Way Into Narnia* (Grand Rapids, Wm. B. Eerdmans, 1979).

Schofield, Stephen, ed. *In Search of C. S. Lewis* (South Plainfield, Bridge Publishing, Inc., 1983).

Schultz, Jeffrey D. and John G. West, Jr., eds. *The C. S. Lewis Readers' Encyclopedia* (Grand Rapids, Zondervan Publishing House, 1998).

Schwartz, Sandford. *C. S. Lewis on the Final Frontier: Science and the Supernatural in the Space Trilogy* (Oxford, Oxford University Press, 2009).

Tandy, Gary L. *The Rhetoric of Certitude: C. S. Lewis's Nonfiction Prose* (Kent, The Kent State University Press, 2009).

Walker, Andrew and James Patrick, eds. *A Christian for All Christians* (Washington, DC, Regnery Gateway, 1992).

Walsh, Chad. *Apostle to the Skeptics* (New York, The Macmillan Co., 1949).

Ward, Michael. *Planet Narnia: The Seven Heavens in the Imagination of C. S. Lewis* (Oxford, Oxford University Press, 2008).

Further reading

Watson, George. *Critical Essays on C. S. Lewis*, Critical Thought
     Series: 1 (Brookfield, Ashgate Publishing Co., 1992).
White, William Luther. *The Image of Man in C. S. Lewis* (Nashville,
     Abingdon Press, 1969).
Zaleski, Philip and Carol Zaleski. *The Fellowship: The Literary Lives
     of the Inklings* (New York, Farrar, Straus and Giroux, 2015).

Other resources

Many journals devoted to Lewis are from Lewis societies. *VII:
     The Journal of the Marion E. Wade Center* and *Sehnsucht*
     <http://www.sehnsucht-cslewis.org>, both noteworthy, are
     exceptions. Of the many websites devoted to Lewis, I have
     chosen seven: these will lead a searcher to others, in some cases
     providing audio and video material as well as bibliographies and
     chronologies, though of the latter the most thorough and exact are
     Hooper's in his *Companion and Guide*, 'A C. S. Lewis Timeline',
     Appendix B in Schultz and West, *The C. S. Lewis Readers'
     Encyclopedia*, and Kilby and Mead's in Warren Lewis's diary,
     Companion and Friends.
<http://www.cslewis.org/resource/lewisrelated/> (The C. S. Lewis
     Foundation).
<http://www.nycslsociety.com/> (The first Lewis society, f. 1969).
<https://www.wheaton.edu/academics/academic-centers/wadecenter/>.
<https://www.oxfordcslewissociety.org/lewis-in-oxford/>.
<http://www.lewissociety.org> (the California C. S. Lewis Society).
<http://nyx.meccahosting.com/~a0008323/> (The Southern
     California C. S. Lewis Society).
<http://www.lewisiana.nl/>.

Publisher's acknowledgements

We are grateful for permission to include the following copyright material in this book.

Extracts from POEMS by C.S. Lewis copyright © C.S. Lewis Pte. Ltd. 1964. Extracts reprinted by permission.

Extract from DYMER by C.S. Lewis copyright © C.S. Lewis Pte. Ltd. Extract reprinted by permission.

Extract from LEARNING IN WAR TIME by C.S. Lewis copyright © C.S. Lewis Pte. Ltd. Extract reprinted by permission.

Extract from BOXEN by C.S. Lewis copyright © C.S. Lewis Pte. Ltd. 1985. Extract reprinted by permission.

Extract from SPIRITS IN BONDAGE by C.S. Lewis copyright © C.S. Lewis Pte. Ltd. Extract reprinted by permission.

Extract from THE PILGRIM'S REGRESS by C.S. Lewis copyright © C.S. Lewis Pte. Ltd. 1933. Extract reprinted by permission.

Extract from AN EXPERIMENT IN CRITICISM by C.S. Lewis copyright © C.S. Lewis Pte. Ltd. Extract reprinted by permission.

The publisher and author have made every effort to trace and contact all copyright holders before publication. If notified, the publisher will be pleased to rectify any errors or omissions at the earliest opportunity.

Index

C. S. Lewis

Index

SOCIAL MEDIA
Very Short Introduction

Join our community
www.oup.com/vsi

- Join us online at the official Very Short Introductions **Facebook** page.
- Access the thoughts and musings of our authors with our online **blog**.
- Sign up for our monthly **e-newsletter** to receive information on all new titles publishing that month.
- Browse the full range of Very Short Introductions online.
- Read **extracts** from the Introductions for free.
- If you are a teacher or lecturer you can order inspection copies quickly and simply via our website.

BESTSELLERS
A Very Short Introduction
John Sutherland

'I rejoice', said Doctor Johnson, 'to concur with the Common Reader.' For the last century, the tastes and preferences of the common reader have been reflected in the American and British bestseller lists, and this *Very Short Introduction* takes an engaging look through the lists to reveal what we have been reading - and why. John Sutherland shows that bestseller lists monitor one of the strongest pulses in modern literature and are therefore worthy of serious study. Along the way, he lifts the lid on the bestseller industry, examines what makes a book into a bestseller, and asks what separates bestsellers from canonical fiction.

'His amiable trawl through the history of popular books is frequently entertaining'

Scott Pack, The Times

www.oup.com/vsi

ENGLISH LITERATURE

A Very Short Introduction

Jonathan Bate

Sweeping across two millennia and every literary genre, acclaimed scholar and biographer Jonathan Bate provides a dazzling introduction to English Literature. The focus is wide, shifting from the birth of the novel and the brilliance of English comedy to the deep Englishness of landscape poetry and the ethnic diversity of Britain's Nobel literature laureates. It goes on to provide a more in-depth analysis, with close readings from an extraordinary scene in King Lear to a war poem by Carol Ann Duffy, and a series of striking examples of how literary texts change as they are transmitted from writer to reader.

{No reviews}

FRENCH LITERATURE
A Very Short Introduction
John D. Lyons

The heritage of literature in the French language is rich, varied, and extensive in time and space; appealing both to its immediate public, readers of French, and also to aglobal audience reached through translations and film adaptations. *French Literature: A Very Short Introduction* introduces this lively literary world by focusing on texts - epics, novels, plays, poems, and screenplays - that concern protagonists whose adventures and conflicts reveal shifts in literary and social practices. From the hero of the medieval *Song of Roland* to the Caribbean heroines of *Tituba, Black Witch of Salem* or the European expatriate in Japan in *Fear and Trembling*, these problematic protagonists allow us to understand what interests writers and readers across the wide world of French.